James Leitch

Practical Educationists And Their Systems of Teaching

James Leitch

Practical Educationists And Their Systems of Teaching

ISBN/EAN: 9783337004965

Printed in Europe, USA, Canada, Australia, Japan

Cover: Foto ©Andreas Hilbeck / pixelio.de

More available books at **www.hansebooks.com**

PRACTICAL EDUCATIONISTS.

Published by

JAMES MACLEHOSE, GLASGOW.

MACMILLAN AND CO., LONDON.

Edinburgh, ... *Edmonston & Douglas.*
Dublin, ... *W. H. Smith & Son.*

MDCCCLXXVI.

PRACTICAL EDUCATIONISTS

AND THEIR

SYSTEMS OF TEACHING.

BY

JAMES LEITCH,

PRINCIPAL OF THE CHURCH OF SCOTLAND NORMAL SCHOOL, GLASGOW.

GLASGOW:
JAMES MACLEHOSE, 61 ST. VINCENT STREET.
Publisher to the University.
1876.

PREFACE.

THIS book is the product of my official duties as Principal of a Normal School, the various Essays being part of a series of lectures delivered by me to the students in training. My object in drawing them up was to give increased interest to the study of education as a science, by connecting its principles with the educationists or teachers who originated them, or first wrought them out successfully in practice. My efforts in this direction have not been suggested by the recent outcry for the instruction of normal students in the science of their adopted profession; but have been carried out during the whole period of my

Principalship, a fact sufficiently proved from the following extract, from the report of the Committee of Council on Education for 1868-69, pp. xxv, 476:—'To the second year's students, the Rector has given a course of formal lectures, on the principles and practice of teaching, with the benefit of all the aid he could derive from some of the best foreign writers on popular education. He adds commonly to the interest of his lecture by connecting the principles of which he speaks with the lives and characters of the men that mainly represent them. The effect is seen in the results of the Christmas examination on school management, which for the last year shews a better percentage for "excellent" or "good," than had been usual before. These lectures of the Rector are occupied exclusively with the methods of tuition which are applicable to all subjects, such being the portion of this extensive subject which he has fitly chosen for himself.'

Each educationist in the series is, so to speak, a representative man, and has more or less left the impress of his personal teaching or principles on English education. Locke brings before us the great public school system of England, and is the chief advocate we have for private education. Pestalozzi is the father of industrial and elementary schools for the people; Bell and Lancaster created the monitorial and subsequent pupil-teacher system, now widely prevalent; Stow displays the fruit of the training system in full maturity; Wilderspin's name is indelibly associated with infant schools; and Spencer is our leading champion for science teaching. Other educationists of equal merit and interest might have been included, but it was necessary to reduce the book to a reasonable size. Should this volume prove serviceable, it may be followed by another.

Prepared with the purpose stated, the papers enter into greater detail than may to the general reader seem desirable: but when it is considered that one object of the book is to enable teachers, from the descriptions given, to apprehend and put into practice methods which in some instances must be quite novel to them, the details may not seem to be out of place. In general, I think, I have confined myself to what is likely to prove useful and interesting to practical teachers; and when it has been at all convenient, I have adopted the plan of letting each author describe his methods in his own words. My own experience and opinions are interspersed throughout, and will prove, it is hoped, a useful addition.

The book will be found to contain, I think, all that is useful and interesting in the systems of the educationists taken up. Each paper has been prepared with the greatest care; and I trust the whole will prove serviceable in saving the time and labour of my brethren, who have a desire to study minutely the principles of their profession—a great many of the books referred to being either out of print, or not readily accessible to the ordinary schoolmaster. At the same time, it will afford me much satisfaction if the perusal of the book stimulate the young teacher to go to the fountain-head and read for himself the works of educationists of this and other countries. It is a study for him of the deepest importance; and the more he reads the richer and rarer will his knowledge become.

The book should also prove of much service to members of school boards interested in the history of education, and in the details of school-method, many points of interest and usefulness to them being fully discussed in its pages. To such of them as are desirous to make themselves familiar with recognized principles of teaching, I can suggest no more interesting way than that by which they are here illustrated. As practical educationists, they will find it beneficial to make themselves acquainted with the best and most advanced results yet reached in education: bearing in mind that "in order to make discoveries that shall help the great cause forward, one must start where the great masters have stopped. The systems of education that have borne sway in the world, the principles on which these systems have been based, their results, and the causes of their successes and failures—all these must be understood by those who are to make any real progress in education. And more than this, a knowledge of what has been done before him puts the student in possession of the best principles for his guidance in administering any system." *

* " Proceedings of the United States National Education Association, 1874," p. 237.

CONTENTS.

JOHN LOCKE.

Chief Events in his life.—What led to the Publication of his "Thoughts on Education"—Character of the Book—Suggestive to Parents as well as Teachers—Deals mainly with the Education of a "Gentleman"—This should be carried on at Home and not at a Public School—His Objections to Public Schools—Cowper's "Tirocinium"—Locke's Estimate of the Character and Work of a Tutor—Physical Education—Rules for the Preservation of Health—Remarks on Moral Discipline—He is opposed to Harsh Measures and to Corporal Punishment—His Suggestions as to suitable Rewards and Punishments—Learning should be made attractive—His plan for Teaching to read—Committing to Memory—Directions as to the Teaching of Writing—Arithmetic—Grammar—Composition—History and Geography—French—Latin—He is against the Prescription of Latin Themes and Verses—Religious Teaching—Dugald Stewart on the "Thoughts"—

The Last Years of Locke's Life—His Versatility as a Writer—Traits in his Character, suggestive to the youthful Teacher.

Pages 1-51.

HENRY PESTALOZZI.

Pestalozzi's Name a "Household Word"—His Early Life and Character—Personal Appearance—He studies first for the Church and afterwards for the Law—Finally decides on Farming—His Love-letter and Marriage—Converts his Farm into an Industrial School—His own Account of its Operation—Reduced to Poverty by the Experiment—Takes to writing Books on Education—"Evening Hour of a Hermit"—"Leonard and Gertrude"—"Mothers' Manuals"—Influence of the French Revolution in Switzerland—Pestalozzi volunteers to teach the Orphans of Stanz—His Experience related in "How Gertrude Teaches Her Children"—Invents the Simultaneous and Monitorial Systems—His Moral Lessons excellent—Originates Object Lessons, their defects—Introduction of Object Lessons into England—Opinion of Professor Moseley on Object Lessons—Pestalozzi's Teaching at Burgdorf—Account by Ramsauer—Pestalozzi's Lessons on Form, Number, and Language—Arithmetic—Pestalozzian Arithmetic introduced into England—He inculcated the Teaching of *Things*, but failed to carry the Principle out in his own Lessons—This is exemplified by his Mode of teaching Geography—Pestalozzi at Buchsee—Contrast between him and De Fellenberg—Pestalozzi at Yverdun—Fichte's Opinion of Pestalozzi and of the "Situation" in Germany—Visit of Karl von Raumer to Yverdun—His Description of Pestalozzi and his Colleagues — Raumer's

Expectations not realised—Pestalozzi's Practice fell far short of his Theories, ... Pages 52-120.

DR. ANDREW BELL.

Sketch of his Life—School at Madras—Invention of the Monitorial System—Letter to Mr. Edgeworth—Publication of an "Experiment on Education"—Full Account of the Monitorial System—Suggestions for its Introduction—Modes of Discipline under this System—Trial by Jury—Example of the Good Effects of Monitorial Discipline—Dr. Bell had the Secret of Successful Teaching—The "Paidometer"—Advantages and Disadvantages of the Monitorial System—Its Chief Advocates quoted—The System Introduced in England—The "Bell and Lancaster" Controversy—Mrs. Trimmer—The System dates further back than either Bell or Lancaster—National Society and British and Foreign School Society Founded—Dr. Bell's Legacies—Chairs of Education in Scottish Universities, ... Pages 121-148.

JOSEPH LANCASTER.

Contrast between the Characters of Bell and Lancaster—Lancaster's Antecedents—His Account of the London Schools of the time—He Opens a School in the Borough Road—Its great Popularity—Lancaster's Monitorial System—System of Teaching Reading—Writing—Arithmetic—His Modes of Discipline—Religious Teaching—Lancaster's Interview with the King—His Prosperity and Extravagance—His Lecturing Tours — He attempts to extend the Monitorial System to

Agriculture — Resigns his Post at the Borough Road—His subsequent Difficulties and Death—Estimate of his Character and Work, ... Pages 149-165.

SAMUEL WILDERSPIN.

Origin of Infant Schools—School at New Lanark, the first Infant School in Great Britain—Others established in London—Wilderspin appointed Master—His first Experiences—Great Success—Called to organize Infant Schools throughout England and Scotland—Death of his Wife, the first Infant School Mistress—Wilderspin in Glasgow and Edinburgh—Status of the Scottish Teacher in his time—Points on which Wilderspin and Stow agree—Wilderspin's Views of what an Infant Teacher should be—His Five Rules for the Guidance of Teachers—The Teacher should follow Nature—Train the Child's Observing Powers by means of Objects—The "Kindergarten" System should be studied along with Wilderspin's—The Ball Frame invented by Wilderspin—Pictures used and recommended by him—The Principle of Combining Amusement with Instruction carried too far in his Rhymes on Weights and Measures—Institution of the Home and Colonial Infant School Society, ... Pages 166-185.

DAVID STOW.

Stow's Attention early directed to Sabbath School Teaching—His Experience in the Saltmarket—He opens a week day Model School—Impetus given to the Opening of similar Institutions in Scotland—Foundation of the first Normal

School—Account of the Early Working of this Institution—
Criticism Lessons—Bible Teaching the great Feature of Stow's
System—Robert Owen's Visit—Foundation of a second
Normal School—The "Training" System illustrated—Distinction between Bible Reading, Bible Teaching, and Bible
Training—Amusing Account by Stow of his Visit to a School
in England—Example of a "Training Lesson"—The "Training System" applied to the Teaching of Science—The Training
System applied to Book-keeping and other Subjects—" Picturing out" Examples—Its use in making "Abstract Lessons"
clear to Children—In "picturing out" Bible Words and
Scenes, the Saviour's Example should be imitated—Example
of a Bible Lesson "pictured out"—System of "picturing out"
inexhaustible—The Sympathy of Numbers—The "Mixed"
System advocated by Stow—Advantages of the "Mixed"
System—Results of this System in America—The conjoint Use
made of the Gallery and Playground in model Training—
Superintendence by Teacher in Playground—Stow's Opinions
on minor School Matters—His Influence on Education,
Pages 186-238.

HERBERT SPENCER.

Spencer would have the Scholastic World revise its Work—His
Estimate of the true "Measure of Value" in Knowledge—
Classification of the leading "Activities" of Life: (*a*) those
which minister to Self-preservation; (*b*) those which are Necessary to gain a Livelihood; (*c*) those which have for their Object
the Rearing and Discipline of Offspring; (*d*) those which are
involved in the Maintenance of proper Social and Political
Relations; (*e*) those which minister to the Tastes and Feelings—

Science best fits a Man for these Spheres of Activity—Science is valuable *per se*, and also as a Means of Discipline—Science *versus* Language—Spencer on Intellectual Education—Old Methods of Teaching are giving place to New—The New should conform to Nature—Teaching should proceed from the Simple to the Complex—Teaching should proceed from the Definite to the Indefinite—Teaching should proceed from the Concrete to the Abstract—The Education of the Child should proceed on the same Principles as the Education of the Race—It should proceed from the Empirical to the Rational—Self-development should be encouraged to the utmost—Education begins in the Cradle—Object Lessons should be given during Childhood and Youth—The Child should be encouraged to Paint and to Draw—The Acquirement of Knowledge should be made Pleasurable—Spencer's Moral Discipline—The Discipline of Natural Consequences—Examples of its Operation—Advantages of this Mode of Discipline—It is the "divinely ordained" Method—Practical Maxims and Rules for Moral Education, ... Pages 239-298.

JOHN LOCKE.

Chief vents in his Life—His " Thoughts on Education"—Character of the Book—Deals mainly with the Education of a "Gentleman"—Objections to Public Schools—Estimate of the Character and Work of a Tutor—Physical Education—Moral Discipline—Opposed to harsh measures—Plan for teaching to Read—As to the teaching of Writing, Arithmetic, &c.—Religious teaching—Traits suggestive to the Youthful Teacher.

JOHN LOCKE, better known as a metaphysician than as an educationist, was born at Wrington, in Somersetshire, in 1632. Of his father nothing noteworthy is recorded, except that he possessed a moderate landed property, and was a captain in the Parliamentary army during the Civil War. Having received his elementary education at Westminster School, Locke entered Christ Church College, Oxford, in 1651, where he was distinguished among his fellow-students by his talents and learning. His nephew and biographer, Lord King, informs us that Locke had in the course of his life the choice of three distinct roads to fortune, and, perhaps, to celebrity; the temptation of con-

A

siderable preferment in the church, the practice of physic as a profession, and the opportunity of engaging in diplomatic employments.

He made choice, in the first place, of the second of these roads, and, after the usual course of preparation, entered upon the practice of medicine, for which he cherished a fondness during his whole life. While practising at Oxford, it was a fortunate circumstance for him that, in 1666, Lord Ashley, afterwards the celebrated Earl of Shaftesbury, came to that city to seek relief from an abscess in his chest, the consequence of a fall from his horse. Locke, happening to be summoned as his attendant, remained with his lordship for some time, and after making himself acquainted with the nature of the complaint, advised that the abscess should be opened, which, as the story goes, was the means of saving the patient's life. From this incident, the well known friendship between the two men took its origin. Lord Ashley invited Locke to reside permanently with him, and would not permit him to practise medicine out of his house, except among some of his particular friends.* From this period a complete change took place, both in the direction of Locke's studies, and in his habits of life. His place of residence was transferred from the uni-

* "Locke and Sydenham," by Dr. John Brown, p. 12.

versity to the metropolis, and from thence he occasionally passed over to the Continent, visiting France, Germany, and Holland, where he had opportunities of profiting by the conversation of some of the most distinguished persons of his age. The last named country was his favourite place of residence, and it was during his exile there in 1687 that he completed his celebrated work, the "Essay concerning Human Understanding," the plan of which had been conceived as early as 1670. Having returned to England soon after the Revolution, he published the first edition of this work in 1690, about the time that Newton published his "Principia," works which contributed to render illustrious the era of the Revolution. Three years later he published his "Thoughts on Education," a subject to which his attention was turned from the circumstance that he was entrusted with directing the studies of Lord Ashley's son, and subsequently of his grandson, the second and third Earls of Shaftesbury respectively, the latter of whom proved to be a man of genius, and is well known in literature as the author of several political and philosophical works, which go collectively under the name of the "Characteristics"; in reference to which book, and to the great exertions of the present representative of this noble family, the seventh Earl, to improve the social condition of the working classes, a *jeu d'esprit*, expressive of the fact that 'humanity is one of Shaftesbury's characteristics,' found currency a few years ago.

Locke, having this onerous duty entrusted to him, was led to examine the ordinary education of the day, and, finding it to be unsatisfactory, he set about making such improvements upon it as he thought necessary; and here I cannot refrain from remarking that, if the study of medicine happily prepared Locke's mind for the study of metaphysics, as Professor Dugald Stewart is of opinion it did, the study of both sciences prepared his mind in an especial manner for the study of education. Written originally in a series of letters to a friend, Locke's book is quaint, and almost gossipy in style, and repeats itself at different places. Published when he had attained the age of sixty, it gives evidence of matured judgment and of ripe experience; the suggestions it contains being of great value, some of them having only of late years begun to make their way. Though the book may seem to modern readers to shine with the borrowed lustre of the author's fame as a writer on philosophy, it was by no means viewed in the same light by his contemporaries. On the contrary, Leibnitz speaks of it as a work of still greater merit than the "Essay on Human Understanding"; and its success was so marked that it ran through several editions in English, and was translated into French, Dutch, and German, and had much influence on education.

In the preface of Locke's book, the following paragraph occurs:—' The well-educating of their children is so much the duty and concern of parents, and the welfare and prosperity of the nation so much depends on it, that I would have every one lay it to heart; and after having well examined and distinguished what fancy, custom, or reason advises in the case, set his helping hand to promote everywhere that way of training up youth, with regard to their several conditions, which is the easiest, shortest, and likeliest to produce virtuous, useful, and able men in their distinct callings; though that most to be taken care of is the gentleman's calling.' * (p. 5.)

This passage, though penned two hundred years ago, might be read with interest in any address to parents, or appeal to the public on behalf of education of modern date. It shows the immense importance which Locke placed on education, concerning which he says in another place,

* "Thoughts on Education." Edited by J. A. St. John. London, 1836. (All references are to this edition.)

'Of all the men we meet with, nine parts of ten are what they are—good or evil, useful or not—by their education; it is that which makes the great difference in mankind.' And his instancing the 'gentleman's calling,' as of first importance, enables me to premise that Locke's treatise bears chiefly on the education or upbringing of a gentleman, and that from the period of infancy, and is on this account not so well suited to the requirements of the elementary teacher; but as it is the duty of a teacher to study the child's *nature*, he will find Locke to be a very suggestive and discreet guide to the knowledge he seeks. To parents also, the book should be specially interesting, a considerable portion of it being addressed quite as much to them as to teachers. Not a few parents may consider the measures it proposes as too harsh, and it probably carries the principle of self-denial too far, or at least farther than would be agreeable to most mothers; but I can assure them that Locke does not make this mistake—if mistake it can be called—from a harshness of disposition, or want of sympathy for children, for he seems to love them with his whole heart, his love manifesting itself in minute solicitude as to their welfare; for example—

'Great care should be taken in waking them,

that it be not done hastily, nor with a loud or shrill voice, or any other sudden violent noise. This often affrights children, and does them great harm; and sound sleep, thus broken off, with sudden alarms, is apt enough to discompose any one. When children are to be wakened out of their sleep, be sure to begin with a low call, and some gentle motion, and so draw them out of it by degrees, and give them none but kind words and usage, until they are come perfectly to themselves, and being quite dressed, you are sure they are thoroughly awake. The being forced from their sleep, how gently soever you do it, is pain enough to them; and care should be taken not to add any other uneasiness to it, especially such that may terrify them.' (p. 37.)

In giving an outline of the book, I shall confine my remarks within the four following divisions—

I. Locke's advocacy of private education.
II. His remarks on physical education.
III. His observations on moral discipline.
IV. His suggestions on subjects to be taught, and how to teach them.

In the first place, then, I have to state that Locke is the chief advocate we have in educational literature for *private* as opposed to *public* education. He is of opinion that the education of a gentleman should be entrusted to a tutor, and be carried on at home, in his father's sight, and not at a public school. His own experience at Westminster had given him a lively sense of the evils prevalent at public schools, where, in the words of Cowper, he had seen—

'The pert made perter, and the tame made wild.'

And being of opinion that virtue and good manners are more important than school learning, and that those in charge of children should study well their natures and aptitudes, a task which is extremely difficult, if not impossible, in large schools, he says,—'I am sure, he who is able to be at the charge of a tutor at home, may there give his son a more genteel carriage, more manly thoughts, and a sense of what is worthy and becoming, with a greater proficiency in learning into the bargain, and ripen him up sooner into a man, than any at school can do. Not that I blame the schoolmaster in this, or think it to be laid to his charge. The difference is great between two or three pupils in the same house, and three or four score boys lodged up and down; for let the master's industry and skill be never so great, it is impossible he should have fifty or an hundred scholars under his eye any longer than they are in the school together: nor can it be expected, that he should instruct them successfully in anything but their books; the forming of their minds and manners requiring a constant attention and particular application to every single boy, which is impossible in a numerous flock, and would be wholly in vain (could he have time to study and correct every one's particular defects, and wrong inclinations), when the lad was to be left to himself, or the prevailing infection of his fellows, the greatest part of the four and twenty hours.' (p. 91.)

And again,—'Till you can find a school, wherein it is possible for the master to look after the manners of his scholars, and can shew as great effects of his care of forming their minds to virtue, and their carriage to good breeding, as of forming their tongues to the learned languages, you must confess that you have a strange value for words, when preferring the languages of the ancient Greeks and Romans to that which made them such brave men, you think it worth while to hazard your son's innocence and virtue for a little Greek and Latin. For, as for that boldness and spirit which lads get amongst their playfellows at school, it has ordinarily such a mixture of rudeness and ill-turned confidence, that those misbecoming and disingenuous ways of shifting in the world must be unlearned, and all the tincture washed out again, to make way for better principles, and such manners as make a truly worthy man. He that considers how diametrically opposite the skill of living well, and managing as a man should do his affairs in the world, is to that malpertness, tricking, or violence learned amongst schoolboys, will think the faults of a more private education infinitely to be preferred to such improvements, and will take care to preserve his child's innocence and modesty at home, as being nearer of kin, and more in the way of those qualities which make a useful and able man.' (pp. 87-8.)

And he would not be afraid of a personal comparison of the results of the rival system.

'Take a boy,' he says, 'from the top of a grammar school, and one of the same age, bred as he should be in his father's family, and bring them into good company together, and then see which of the two will have the more manly carriage, and address himself with the more becoming assurance to strangers. Here, I imagine, the schoolboy's confidence will either fail or discredit him; and if it be such as fits him only for the conversation of boys, he were better to be without it.' (p. 92.)

The evils which Locke charges against public schools, are, I believe, by no means exaggerated, and are worthy of serious attention. The public school with which he was acquainted, and which he had in view when he wrote, was similar to Rugby, Harrow, Eton, and Winchester Schools at the present time, where hundreds of boys, sent from greater or less distances, lodge together under the same roof, and receive instruction. The cruelties which the boys inflict, one upon the other, especially the strong upon the weak, when the eyes of the masters are not upon them, have formed the subject of public comment and literary effort from time to time, *e.g.*, the recent exposure of 'tunding' at Winchester, and the graphic account of 'fagging' in "Tom Brown's School Days." About a hundred years after Locke, Cowper wrote a poem of nearly one thousand lines against the system which, as he was also a pupil of Westminster, it is interesting to peruse along with the "Thoughts." It is entitled "Tirocinium," and contains a bitter denunciation of the practice of sending boys to public schools. 'Why,' he exclaims,—

'Why then resign into a stranger's hand
A task as much within your own command ;
That God and nature, and your interest too,
Seem with one voice to delegate to you?
Why hire a lodging in a house unknown
For one whose tenderest thoughts all hover round your
    own?'

For the teachers he has no respect, calling them—

> 'Public hackneys in the schooling trade,
> Who feed a pupil's intellect with store
> Of syntax truly, but with little more.'

And he will listen to no arguments in favour of the public system, even though instances be adduced of school bred boys remaining virtuous.

> 'Such rare exceptions, shining in the dark,
> Prove rather than impeach the just remark,
> As here and there a twinkling star descried
> Serves but to shew how black is all beside.'

Important testimony to the same effect is borne by the late Dr. Arnold, of Rugby, who, though one of the most successful head-masters of a public school, was fully alive to the evils of the system. In writing to a friend on the subject, he acknowledges that it would be with fear and trembling that he should send his own sons to a public school; and confesses that a very good private tutor would tempt him to try private education.*

It is worthy of note that, about the time Cowper's poem was published, an extraordinary example occurred in public life of the truth of the theory of education, held in common by

* Stanley's "Life of Arnold," p. 330.

Locke and Cowper, and which is beyond question the best example that can be adduced in favour of home education. I refer to the case of the younger Pitt, who became prime minister of England at the age of twenty-four, a result solely to be accounted for by the fact that he was educated at home, and not at school, and had constantly before him the example of his distinguished father, who proved to him the best of schoolmasters. I am indebted for this example to a lecture on the "Two Pitts," delivered at Glasgow in January, 1874, by Professor Seeley of Cambridge.

Even if we were to yield to the influence of Locke's reasoning, and of Cowper's rhetoric on this subject, we should be obliged to confess that private tuition, however well suited for the sons and daughters of parents in the upper classes of society, could never overtake the education of the children of the poor, and can never to any extent be adopted as a means of national education. The system proposed by Locke, therefore, need not be refuted here. A serious objection to its adoption appears to me to lie in the fact that, however preferable a home education might be for securing the end Locke had in view, the average child, so brought up, would lack that healthy stimulus to learning only to be had in its purity and strength in the presence of other children; and if the large middle-class schools of England were re-modelled, so that boys might attend them, and still be subject to home influences (their removal from which seems to me to be the origin of the evil); and further, if girls were admitted to these schools on the same footing as boys, the evils complained of by Locke would be remedied in a great degree. As I will shew more fully in my chapter on David Stow, the mixed system tends to improve boys in manners, language, and personal habits, while girls on the other hand receive corresponding benefit. This system has been fairly tried in the large schools of America, and been attended with complete success.

Locke's estimate of the character and work of a tutor is, as may be guessed, very high. His first qualifications are breeding and knowledge of the world.

['The great work of a governor,' he says, ' is to fashion the carriage and form the mind; to settle in his pupil good habits, and the principles of virtue and wisdom; to give him by little and little a view of mankind, and work him into a love and imitation of what is excellent and praiseworthy; and in the prosecution of it to give him vigour, activity, and industry. The studies which he sets him upon are but as it were the exercises of his faculties and employment of his time, to keep him from sauntering and idleness, to teach him application, and accustom him to take pains, and to give him some little taste of what his own industry must perfect. For who expects that under a tutor a young gentleman should be an accomplished critic, orator, or logician? go to the bottom of metaphysics, natural philosophy, or mathematics? or be a master in history or chronology? though something of each of these is to be taught him; but it is only to open the door that he may look in, and as it were begin an acquaintance, but not to dwell there, and a governor would be much blamed that should keep his pupil too long, and lead him too far in most of them.(But of good breeding, knowledge of the world, virtue, industry, and a love of reputation, he cannot have too much;) and if he have these, he will not long want what he needs or desires of the other. And since it cannot be hoped he should have time and strength to learn all things, most pains should be taken about that which is most necessary; and that principally looked after which will be of most and frequentest use to him in the world.' (pp. 140-41.)

In answer to the Earl of Peterborough, who

had applied to him to recommend a tutor for his son, he says, 'I must beg leave to own that I differ a little from your Lordship in what you propose; your Lordship would have a thorough scholar, and I think it not much matter whether he be any great scholar or no; if he but understand Latin well, and have a general scheme of the sciences, I think that enough; but I would have him well bred, well tempered, a man that, having been conversant with the world, and amongst men, would have great application in observing the humour and genius of my Lord your son; and omit nothing that might help to form his mind, and dispose him to virtue, knowledge, and industry. This I look upon as the great business of a tutor; this is putting life into his pupil, which, when he has got, masters of all kinds are easily to be had; for, when a young gentleman has got a relish of knowledge, the love and credit of doing well spurs him on; he will, with or without teachers, make great advances in whatever he has a mind to. Mr. Newton learned his mathematics only of himself; and another friend of mine Greek without a master; though both these studies seem more to require the help of a tutor than any other.'*

Locke's advice to the parent is to spare no

* Lord King's "Life of Locke," p. 8.

care nor cost to find such a tutor, for he that can procure a tutor that will train his child's mind to virtue, and his manners to good breeding, makes a better purchase for the child than if he had laid out the money on the purchase of more acres. Cowper is urgent in offering similar advice, and is equally alive to the difficulties of finding such a man.

> ' But having found him, be thou duke or earl,
> Show thou hast sense enough to prize the pearl,
> And as thou wouldst the advancement of thine heir
> In all good faculties beneath his care,
> Respect, as is but rational and just,
> A man deemed worthy of so dear a trust.'

II. It does not surprise one to find that Locke, having prepared himself for the practice of medicine, and being fully alive to the great blessings of health and strength, from the fact that his own health through life was very delicate, and required constant care, places great importance on physical training, and begins his work with it, remarking—'Though our chief care should be about the inside (the child's mind), yet the clay-cottage is not to be neglected. I shall, therefore, begin with the *case*, and consider, First, the health of the body.'

On this subject, Locke's book contains a store of valuable precepts, on such subjects as air, diet, sleep, clothing, daily habits, &c., which I strongly advise every teacher to make his own.

Physical training does not directly fall within the sphere of an elementary teacher's duties; yet I hold it to be essential that he should make himself acquainted with the laws of health, that he should strive to obey them himself, and, when it lies in his power, that he should teach his pupils to know and obey them. And the Committee of Council, by introducing drill into their educational programme, indicate that, in their opinion, it is the duty of the schoolmaster to lend a helping hand in the physical training of the children of the nation. Without entering into details, Locke's rules for the preservation of health are thus summed up:—'Plenty of open air, exercise, and sleep; plain diet, no wine or strong drink, and very little or no physic; not too warm and strait clothing; especially the head and feet kept cold, and the feet often used to cold water, and exposed to wet.' (p. 44.)

If any exception were taken to these simple and easily observable rules, it would certainly be to the last; the modern maxim being, "Keep the head cool, and the feet warm," a safer rule than Locke's by far. Indeed, a careful perusal of the book will enable the student to perceive that Locke errs on the side of recommending overly-harsh physical measures, such as would be apt to send delicate children to early graves. He says,—'I would also advise his feet to be washed every day in cold water, and to have his shoes so thin that they might leak and let in water whenever he comes near it.' (p. 13.)

The practice common in country districts and in poor families of allowing children to run barefoot, except in very hard weather, is certainly preferable to that recommended here. The carrying out of these rules, however, in the case of his own ward, is said to have been successful; Lord Ashley, a delicate youth, having become, under Locke's directions, a strong man.

III. On the subject of moral discipline, Locke's remarks are invaluable, and should be thoughtfully studied by every teacher. In opening the subject he says very truly and beautifully— 'Due care being had to keep the body in strength and vigour, so that it may be able to obey and execute the orders of the mind; the next and principal business is to set the mind right, that on all occasions it may be disposed to consent to nothing but what may be suitable to the dignity and excellency of a rational creature.' (p. 44.) And again—'As the strength of the body lies chiefly in being able to endure hardships, so also does that of the mind.

And the great principle and foundation of all virtue and worth is placed in this, that a man is able to deny himself his own desires, cross his own inclinations, and purely follow what reason directs as best, though the appetite lean the other way.' (p. 45.)

It is the duty of parents, therefore, to train their children to self-denial when 'their minds are most tender, most easy to be bowed'; for if it is delayed till the children are grown up, it may be too late to 'get out those weeds which their own hands have planted, and which have taken too deep a root to be easily extirpated. For he that hath been used to have his will in everything, as long as he was in coats, why should we think it strange that he should desire it and contend for it still when he is in breeches.' (p. 46).

The child, then, when he is young, must be taught to submit his will to the reason of others, otherwise he cannot be expected to submit to his own reason when he is of an age to make use of it. This teaching should begin before the child leaves its cradle.

'The first thing children should learn to know should be, that they were not to have anything because it pleased them, but because it was thought fit for them. If they were never suffered to obtain their desire by the impatience they expressed for it, they would no more cry for other things than they do for the moon.' (p. 53.) Illustrations of this truth, he says, are common.

'I have seen children at a table, who, whatever was there, never asked for anything, but contentedly took what was given them; and, at another place, I have seen others cry for everything they saw, must be served out of every dish, and that first, too. What made this vast difference but this, that one was accustomed to have what they called or cried for, the other to go without it? The younger they are, the less, I think, are their unruly and disorderly appetites to be complied with; and the less reason they have of their own, the more are they to be under the absolute power and restraint of those in whose hands they are. From which, I confess it will follow, that none but discreet people should be about them.' (pp. 53-4.) When the child gets up in years, however, he should be admitted nearer to the parent's familiarity, 'so shall you have him your obedient subject when he is a child, and your affectionate friend when he is a man.' In giving this advice, Locke seems to have drawn upon his own experience in childhood, his father, of whom he always spoke with great respect and affection, having exacted the utmost deference from his son in the early part of his life, but gradually treated him with less and less reserve, as he grew up.* If such a course is pursued, a child will receive from his early education some influence that will sway his life, and acquire habits that will be woven into the very principles of his nature.

With respect to the manner in which this early discipline is to be carried out, it is only due to Locke to say that he is quite opposed to severity. The child must be taught self-denial, but not by harsh measures.

'Great severity of punishment,' he says, 'does but very little good—nay, great harm in education; and I believe it will be found that, *ceteris paribus*, those children who have been most chastised, seldom make the best men.' (p. 57.)

Care must be taken, therefore, that the child's mind be not curbed, nor humbled too much, by too strict a hand being kept over it. The subjection desired should, if possible, be attained by moral means.

'He that has found a way how to keep up a child's spirits, easy, active, and free, and yet at the same time to restrain him from many things he has a mind to, and to draw him to things that are uneasy to him; he, I say, that knows how to reconcile these seeming contradictions has, in my

* Lord King's *Life of Locke*, p. 2.

opinion, got the true secret of education. The usual, lazy, and short way by chastisement and the rod, which is the only instrument of government that tutors generally know, or ever think of, is the most unfit of any to be used in education.' (p. 59.)

For if our discipline merely succeed in inspiring children with a dread of bodily pain, what a despicable motive this is to govern their actions and direct their conduct.

'I cannot think, therefore,' he says, 'that any correction is useful to a child where the shame of suffering for having done amiss does not work more upon him than the pain.' (p. 60.)

On this point Locke undoubtedly influenced the opinions of Stow.

What the teacher should aim at, accordingly, in administering corporal punishment, should not be to inflict a requisite amount of bodily pain, but to create a sense of shame in the mind of the culprit. I am of opinion, therefore, that the practice adopted by some teachers, of taking a boy into a side room, and there flogging him, is quite indefensible; as also the practice of putting a file of boys into a corner of the school-room, and there directing a volley of 'palmies' at them in an off-hand way. Corporal punishment, when it is resorted to at all, should be inflicted publicly, and in a serious manner, the eyes of the whole school being turned on the offender, in which case a feeling of shame is almost certain to be aroused. But it may be said that there are instances, in which it seems almost necessary to inflict bodily pain *per se* as a means of correction. These, I trust, are rare, and I would by all means advise the teacher to resort to expulsion rather than degrade his own moral character and that of the school by flogging boys into submission. To have even one pupil of such a stamp may win for the indiscreet teacher the character of a 'plagosus Orbilius' (Horace, *Epistles*, 2nd book, i, 70), who, in the words of Fuller, 'mars more scholars than he makes.' While Locke is clearly of opinion that all moral means at the teacher's disposal should be exhausted in the first place, he admits that there is one fault for which children should be beaten, and that is obstinacy or rebellion.

'And in this, too,' he says, 'I would have it ordered so, if it can be, that the shame of the whipping, and not the pain, should be the greatest part of the punishment. Shame of doing amiss, and deserving chastisement, is the only true restraint belonging to virtue. The smart of the rod, if shame accompanies it not, soon ceases and is forgotten; and will quickly by use lose its terror.

I have known the children of a person of quality kept in awe by the fear of having their shoes pulled off, as much as others by apprehensions of a rod hanging over them. Some such punishment I think better than beating; for it is shame of the fault, and the disgrace that attends it, that they should stand in fear of rather than pain, if you would have them have a temper truly ingenuous.' (pp. 104-5.)

Further, he observes that punishment should never be accompanied by an outburst of anger; and in inculcating 'judiciousness in punishment,' he says—'This, I confess, requires something more than setting children a task, and whipping them without any more ado, if it be not done and done to our fancy. This requires care, attention, observation, and a nice study of children's tempers, and weighing their faults well, before we come to this sort of punishment;' an observation which every teacher should lay to heart.

The teacher should be sparing in his correction for the best of all reasons, that it is his business to create a liking for learning, and, as Locke says, ' Children come to hate things which were at first acceptable to them, when they find themselves whipped, and chid, and teased about them. Offensive circumstances ordinarily affect innocent things

which they are joined with, and the very sight of a cup wherein any one uses to take nauseous physic turns his stomach, so that nothing will relish well out of it, though the cup be never so clean and well shaped, and of the richest materials.' (p. 61.)

Frequent correction, then, should be carefully avoided; the strap or cane should on no account be seen lying *in terrorem* on the teacher's desk or table; and instead of taking for his model Goldsmith's schoolmaster,

'A man severe he was, and stern to view,'

or imitating the example of Hood's Irish schoolmaster who kept his children

'Sitting like timid hares, all trembling on their forms,'

the teacher should cultivate gentleness of manner towards his pupils, and while he strives by a combination of mildness and firmness to secure a due measure of respect towards himself, he should carefully avoid creating in their minds any feeling of fear or terror. As Locke beautifully says,—'It is impossible children should learn anything whilst their thoughts are possessed and disturbed with any passion, especially fear, which makes the strongest impression on their yet tender and weak spirits. Keep the mind in an easy calm temper, when you would have it receive your instructions, or any increase of knowledge. It is as impossible to draw fair and regular characters on a trembling mind, as on a shaking paper.' (p. 256.)

Locke's remarks remind me of Cowper's lines on Discipline, which he personifies as a sage who dwelt,

> ' In colleges and halls in ancient days,
> When learning, virtue, piety, and truth
> Were precious, and inculcated with care.
> His eye was meek and gentle, and a smile
> Played on his lips ; and in his speech was heard
> Paternal sweetness, dignity, and love.
> The occupation dearest to his heart
> Was to encourage goodness; learning grew
> Beneath his care a thriving vigorous plant.'

On the other hand, Locke is of opinion that flattery and rewards of things that are pleasant should not be made use of in education.

'He that will give to his son apples or sugar-plums, or what else of this kind he is most delighted with, to make him learn his book, does but authorize his love of pleasure, and cocker up that dangerous propensity, which he ought by all means to subdue, and stifle in him. To make a good, a wise, and a virtuous man, it is fit he should learn to cross his appetite, and deny his inclination to riches, finery, or pleasing his palate, &c., whenever his reason advises the contrary, and his duty requires it. But when you draw him to do anything that is fit by the offer of money, or reward the pains of learning his book by the pleasure of a luscious morsel; when you promise him a lace cravat, or a fine new suit, upon performance of some of his little tasks, what do you, by proposing these as rewards, but allow them to be the good things he should aim at, and thereby encourage his longing for them, and accustom him to place his happiness in them?' (p. 63.)

What then shall we propose to ourselves as suitable rewards and punishments for children? and Locke grants that rewards and punishments should be proposed. We shall give our author's answer in his own words:—'The rewards and punishments then, whereby we should keep children in order, are quite of another kind, and of that force, that when we can get them once to work, the business, I think, is done, and the difficulty is over. Esteem and disgrace are, of all others, the most powerful incentives to the mind, when once it is brought to relish them. If you can once get into children a love of credit, and an apprehension of shame and disgrace, you have put into them the true principle, which will constantly work, and incline them to the right. But it will be asked, How shall this be done? I confess it does not, at first appearance, want some difficulty; but yet I think it worth our while to seek the ways (and practise them when found) to attain this, which I look on as the great secret of education.

'*First*, children (earlier, perhaps, than we think) are very sensible of praise and commendation. They find a pleasure in being esteemed and valued, especially by their parents, and those whom they depend on. If, therefore, the father caress and commend them when they do well, show a cold and neglectful countenance to them upon doing ill, and this, accompanied by a like carriage of the mother and all others that are about them, it will, in a little time, make them sensible of the difference; and this, if constantly observed, I doubt not, but will, of itself, work more than threats or blows, which lose their force when once grown common, and are of no use when shame does not attend them; and, therefore, are to be forborne, and never to be used, but in the case hereafter mentioned, when it is brought to extremity.

'But, *secondly*, to make the sense of esteem or disgrace sink the deeper, and be of the more weight, other agreeable or disagreeable things should constantly accompany these different states; not as particular rewards and punishments of this or that particular action, but as necessarily belonging to, and constantly attending one who, by his carriage, has brought himself into a state of disgrace or commendation. By which way of treating them, children may as much as possible be brought to conceive that those that are commended, and in esteem for doing well, will necessarily be beloved and cherished by every body, and have all other good things as a consequence of it ; and, on the other side, when any one by miscarriage falls into disesteem, and cares not to preserve his credit, he will unavoidably fall under neglect and contempt, and in that state, the want of whatever might satisfy or delight him will follow. In this way the objects of their desires are made assisting to virtue, when a settled experience from the beginning teaches children that the things they delight in belong to, and are to be enjoyed by those only who are in a state of reputation. If, by these means, you can come once to shame them out of their faults (for besides that, I would willingly have no punishment), and make them in love with the pleasure of being well thought of, you may turn them as you please, and they will be in love with all the ways of virtue.' (pp. 66-8.)

I may conclude the section on moral discipline by stating that Locke recommends that curiosity in children, "which is but an appetite after knowledge, should be carefully encouraged, and kept busy and active." (1) Do not check nor discountenance any inquiries he shall make, nor suffer them to be laughed at; but answer all his questions, and explain the matter he desires to know. His mind will thus insensibly expand; for knowledge is grateful to the understanding, as light to the eyes. (2) Take care that children never receive deceitful or deluding answers. (3) Perhaps it may not sometimes be amiss to excite their curiosity, by bringing strange and new things in their way on purpose to engage their inquiry.

IV. I now come to the fourth and last division of my subject—viz., the subjects that Locke recommends for study, and the methods he suggests for teaching them. Though in enumerating the chief requisites of a gentleman's education, he gives preference to them in the following order—virtue, wisdom, good-breeding, and learning—he is very desirous that learning, though kept subservient to higher qualities, should be acquired in a proper way, and to a considerable extent. And to shew that the art of teaching is with him a matter of the greatest importance, I need only quote the following remark:—
'The great skill of a teacher is to get, and keep, the attention of his scholar; whilst he

has that, he is sure to advance as fast as the learner's abilities will carry him; and without that, all his bustle and bother will be to little or no purpose. To attain this, he should make the child comprehend (as much as may be) the usefulness of what he teaches him, and let him see by what he has learnt that he can do something which he could not before; something, which gives him some power and real advantage above others who are ignorant of it. To this, he should add sweetness in all his instructions; and by a certain tenderness in his whole carriage, make the child sensible that he loves him, and designs nothing but his good, the only way to beget love in the child, which will make him hearken to his lessons, and relish what he teaches him.' (pp. 256-57.)

And, in the following passages, he enjoins not only the necessity of interesting his pupils, but of varying his lessons in a suitable way:—
'The natural temper of children disposes their minds to wander—novelty alone takes them; whatever that presents, they are presently eager to have a taste of, and are as soon satisfied with it. They quickly grow weary of the same thing, and so have almost their whole delight in change and variety. It is a contradiction to the natural state of childhood for them to fix their fleeting thoughts. Whether this be owing to the temper

of their brains, or the quickness or instability of their animal spirits, over which the mind has not yet got a full command; this is visible, that it is a pain to children to keep their thoughts steady to any thing. A lasting continued attention is one of the hardest tasks can be imposed on them; and, therefore, he that requires their application, should endeavour to make what he proposes as grateful and agreeable as possible.' (pp. 254-55.) Through all Locke's directions about teaching, there runs this advice, to make the subject as attractive as possible, and to combine instruction with amusement. Hear what he says on the teaching of *reading*:—'When the child can talk, it is time he should begin to learn to read. But as to this, give me leave here to inculcate again what is very apt to be forgotten—viz., that great care is to be taken that it be never made as a business to him, nor he look on it as a task. I have always had a fancy that learning might be made a play and recreation to children, and that they might be brought to desire to be taught, if it were proposed to them as a thing of honour, credit, delight and recreation, or as a reward for doing something else. . . . Children should not have anything like work, or serious, laid on them; neither their minds nor their bodies will bear it. It injures their healths;

and their being forced and tied down to their books, in an age at enmity with all such restraint, has, I doubt not, been the reason why a great many have hated books and learning all their lives after.' (pp. 229-31.)

He accordingly suggests contrivances for teaching children to read, whilst they think they are only playing, and instances examples of the success of such contrivances.

'I know a person of great quality (more yet to be honoured for his learning and virtue than for his rank and high place), who, by pasting on the six vowels (for in our language *y* is one) on the six sides of a die, and the remaining eighteen consonants on the sides of three other dice, has made this a play for his children, that *he* shall win who, at one cast, throws most words on these four dice; whereby his eldest son, yet in coats, has played himself into spelling with great eagerness, and without once having been chid for it, or forced to it.' (p. 233.)

'When by these gentle ways he begins to be able to read, some easy pleasant book, suited to his capacity, should be put into his hands, wherein the entertainment that he finds might draw him on, and reward his pains in reading. To this purpose, I think "Æsop's Fables" the best, which being stories apt to delight and entertain a child, may yet afford useful reflections to a grown man; and if his memory retain them all his life after, he will not repent to find them there, amongst his manly thoughts and serious business. If his Æsop has pictures in it, it will entertain him much the better, and encourage him to read, when it carries the increase of knowledge with it; for such visible objects children hear talked of in vain, and without any satisfaction, whilst they have no ideas of them; those ideas being not to be had from sounds, but from the things themselves, or their pictures. And therefore I think, as soon as he begins to spell, as many pictures of animals should be got him as can be found, with the printed names to them, which at the same time will invite him to read, and afford him matter of inquiry and knowledge. And if those about him will talk to him often about the stories he has read, and hear him tell them, it will, besides other advantages, add encouragement and delight to his reading when he finds there is some use and pleasure in it. These baits seem wholly neglected in the ordinary method, and it is usually long before learners find any use or pleasure in reading, which may tempt them to it, and so take books only for fashionable amusements or impertinent troubles, good for nothing.' (pp. 236-38.)

Locke's recommendations about reading-books shew that he was far ahead of the practice of his age; indeed, it is only of late years that views, similar to his own, have been carried out in the many excellent series now offered to the public. In connection with reading there is a good and useful practice now adopted in many schools—viz., of making the children commit to memory noteworthy passages both in prose and poetry; but Locke informs us that he sees no use in this at all. And he disposes of the usual argument in favour of the practice in the following way:—
'I hear it is said that children should be employed in getting things by heart to exercise and improve their memories. I could wish this were said with as much authority of reason as it is with forwardness of assurance, and that this practice were established upon good observation more than old custom; for it is evident that strength of memory is owing to a happy constitution, and not to any habitual improvement got by exercise.' (p. 274.)

In this respect he is undoubtedly wrong; but I suspect he has chiefly in view the learning of passages from Greek and Latin authors, though his intention is by no means clear. He thinks, however, that boys should commit to memory passages which are worth remembrance; and

' such wise and useful sentences being once given in charge to their memories, they should never be suffered to forget again, but be often called to account for them ; whereby, besides the use these sayings may be to them in their future life, as so many good rules and observations, they will be taught to reflect often, and bethink themselves what they have to remember, which is the only way to make the memory quick and useful.' (p. 277.)

Whatever exception may be taken to the committing of prose, few will deny that the learning of poetry cultivates the taste, and enables the child to acquire choice words, and to become familiar with beautiful thoughts. On this account, I am of opinion that children should begin to learn verses as soon as they can read with fluency. Locke's opinion may, in a great measure, have been influenced by the fact that he was quite insensible to the beauties of poetry, and held in abhorrence the poetic art, expressing it as his opinion that 'a father who wishes his son a poet must surely desire to have him bid defiance to all other callings and business.'

I now proceed to give Locke's directions as to the teaching of *writing*, and on this subject I have to remark, that the practice introduced by the Revised Code, and now universal in schools, of carrying on reading, writing, and ciphering together, from the time of the child's entrance into school, is ahead of Locke's system. He says, 'When a child *can read English well* it will be seasonable to enter him in writing.'

After giving directions about holding the pen, and placing the arm and body to the paper, he goes on to say,—' These practices being got over, the way to teach him to write without much trouble, is to get a plate graved with the characters of such a hand as you like best; but you must remember to have them a pretty deal bigger than he should ordinarily write; for every one naturally comes by degrees to write a less hand than he at first was taught, but never a bigger. Such a plate being graved, let several sheets of good writing paper be printed off with red ink, which he has nothing to do but go over with a good pen filled with black ink, which will quickly bring his hand to the formation of those characters, being at first shewed where to begin, and how to form every letter. And when he can do that well, he must then exercise on fair paper, and so may easily be brought to write the hand you desire.' (p. 242.)

Locke, it will be observed, is the originator of the traced line system which is generally adopted in school copies at the present time. And as drawing and writing now usually go hand in hand in the best schools, I cannot forbear quoting Locke's well-deserved encomium on the usefulness of the former art :—' When he can write well and quick, I think it may be convenient not only to continue the exercise of his hand in writing, but also to improve the use of it further in drawing— a thing very useful to a gentleman in several occasions, but especially if he travel, as that which helps a man often to express in a few lines well put together, what a whole sheet of paper in writing would not be able to represent and make intelligible. How many buildings may a man see, how many machines and habits meet with, the ideas whereof would be easily retained and communicated by a little skill in drawing, which, being committed to words, are in danger to be lost, or, at best, but ill retained in the most exact descriptions! I do not mean that I would have your son a perfect painter; to be that to any tolerable degree will require more time than a young gentleman can spare from his other improvements of greater moment. But so much insight into perspective and skill in drawing as will enable him to represent tolerably on paper anything he sees, except faces, may, I think, be got in a little time, especially if he have a genius to it; but when that is wanting, unless it be in things absolutely necessary, it is better to let him pass them by quietly, than to vex him about them to no purpose; and therefore in this, as in all other things not absolutely necessary, the rule holds, *Nil invitâ Minervâ.*' (pp. 242-44.)

In the matter of *arithmetic* Locke offers no practical suggestions, contenting himself with saying, 'Arithmetic is of so general use in all parts of life and business, that scarce anything is to be done without it. This is certain, a man cannot have too much of it, nor too perfectly; he should therefore begin to be exercised in counting as soon and as far as he is capable of it, and do something in it every day, till he is master of the art of numbers.' (p. 280.)

On the kindred subject of *book-keeping*, he expresses his strong sense of its usefulness: 'It is seldom observed that he who keeps an account of his income and expenses, and thereby has constantly under view the course of his domestic affairs, lets them run to ruin; and I doubt not but many a man gets behind hand before he is aware, or runs further on when he is once in, for want of this care or the skill to do it. I would therefore advise all gentlemen to learn perfectly merchants' accounts.' (p. 324.)

This advice is equally valuable to men of all ranks and professions, and Locke adds to its value by recommending the father to require his son to keep all the home accounts, as soon as he has acquired sufficient skill to undertake the task.

On the subject of *grammar*, Locke expresses himself strongly and sensibly against the practice of taking up the time of boys with Greek and Latin grammar when the grammar of their own tongue is never proposed to them as worthy of their care and attention. In respect to foreign languages, he considers that learning them by rote would serve well enough for the common affairs of life and ordinary commerce, instancing the fact that many express themselves quite properly in the English tongue, who have received no instruction in the grammar of the language; and after this expression of opinion we are not surprised to hear from him that if grammar ought to be taught at any time, it must be to one that can speak the language already; (p. 264); an opinion strongly shared in by Herbert Spencer. His partiality for practical skill is still further apparent in his observations on '*style*,' or, as we usually term it, '*composition.*'

'It might not be amiss,' he says, 'to make children, as soon as they are capable of it, often tell a story of anything they know; and to correct at first the most remarkable fault they are guilty of, in their way of putting it together. When that fault is cured, then to shew them the next, and so on, till one after another all, at least the gross ones, are mended. When they can tell tales pretty well, then it may be the time to make them write them.' (p. 292.)

This suggestion seems to have met with recognition in the compilation of the standards of examination proposed by the Education Department. Still further to practise them in composition, he goes on to say—"When they understand how to write English, with due connection, propriety, and order, and are pretty well masters of a tolerable narrative style, they may be advanced to writing of letters; wherein they should not be put upon any strains of wit or compliment, but taught to express their own plain easy sense, without any incoherence, confusion or roughness. The writing of letters has so much to do in all the occurrences of human life, that no gentleman can avoid shewing himself in this kind of writing. Occasions will daily force him to make use of his pen, which besides the consequences that in his affairs, his well or ill managing of it often draws after it, always lays him open to a severer examination of his breeding, sense, and abilities, than oral discourses; whose transient faults, dying for the most part with the sound that gives them life, and so not subject to a strict review, more easily escape observation and censure.' (pp. 293-94.)

On *history* and *geography* as branches of learning, there is nothing noteworthy in Locke's pages, but in the matter of *languages* he is very explicit and minute. A gentleman should study his own language in the first instance; but, if he has time to go further, he should by all means acquire a knowledge of French, Latin, and Greek. French, he thinks, should be taken up first.

'As soon as he can speak English, it is time for him to learn some other language. This nobody doubts of when French is proposed. And the reason is because people are accustomed to the right way of teaching that language, which is by talking it into children in constant conversation, and not by grammatical rules. The Latin tongue would easily be taught the same way if his tutor, being constantly with him, would talk nothing else to him, and make him answer still in the same language. But because French is a living language, and to be used more in speaking, that should be first learned, that the yet pliant organs of speech might be accustomed to a due formation of those sounds, and he get the habit of pronouncing French well, which is the harder to be done the longer it is delayed.' (pp. 246-47.)

After French should come Latin—a language which he looks upon as absolutely necessary to a *gentleman;* but at the same time he reminds his readers that nothing can be more ridiculous than that a father should waste his own money and his son's time, in setting him to learn Latin when he designs him for a trade. (p. 247.) And how applicable are the following remarks to the practice in country schools at the present day :—
'Could it be believed, unless we had everywhere amongst us examples of it, that a child should be forced to learn the rudiments of a language which he is never to use in the course of life that he is designed to, and neglect all the while the writing a good hand, and casting accounts, which are of great advantage in all conditions of life, and to most trades indispensably necessary? But, though these qualifications, requisite to trade and commerce, and the business of the world, are seldom or never to be had at grammar schools, yet thither, not only gentlemen send their younger sons, intended for trades, but even tradesmen and farmers fail not to send their children, though they have neither intention nor ability to make them scholars. If you ask them why they do this, they think it as strange a question as if you should ask them why they go to church. Custom serves for reason, and has, to

those who take it for reason, so consecrated this method, that it is almost religiously observed by them, and they stick to it as if their children had scarce an orthodox education unless they lear'ed Lilly's Grammar.' (pp. 248-49.)

This practice is, happily, not an unmixed evil, inasmuch as the mental training acquired in the getting up of the dead language is a good thing in itself; but equally beneficial training can be obtained in the study of a modern language, which has the double advantage of being serviceable in after-life. On this subject I confess that my sympathies are very much with Locke; and to let it be seen that there is no prejudiced element in these sympathies, I frankly acknowledge that I spent more time over the acquirement of Greek and Latin, in my course at the university, and in subsequent study, than over any other branch of learning with which my attention has been engaged.

'In regard to the method of teaching Latin, Locke is in favour of its being carried on by talking and reading. Trouble the child with no grammar at all, but let him learn Latin as he does French :—' If, therefore, a man could be got who, himself speaking good Latin, would always be about your son, talk constantly to him, and suffer him to speak or read nothing else, this would be the true and genuine way, and that which I would propose, not only as the easiest and best, wherein a child might, without pains or chiding, get a languag which others are wont to be whipt for at school six or seven years together.' (p. 250.)

If such a man cannot be got, the next best course is to have the child taught 'by taking some easy and pleasant book, such as "Æsop's Fables," and writing the English translation (made as literal as it can be) in one line, and the Latin words which answer each of them just over it in another. These let him read every day over and over again, till he perfectly understands the Latin, and then go on to another fable, till he be also perfect in that, not omitting what he is already perfect in, but sometimes reviewing that, to keep it in his memory.' (p. 251.)

We hear Jacotot's voice, a century later, inculcating the same method, and practising it at Louvain, in drilling the young Flemings into a knowledge of French.

Locke shows his good sense in denouncing the practice of giving boys Latin themes and verses to write; and he enjoins the parent to obtain for his son exemption from this infliction by all the means in his power, 'insisting, if it will do any good, that you have no design to make him either a Latin orator or poet.'

'If boys' inventions are to be quickened by such exercise,' he adds, 'let them make themes in English where they have facility and a command of words, and will better see what kind of thoughts they have when put into their own language.'

Locke's first method of teaching Latin is no doubt borrowed from Montaigne, an educationist whose ideas he has absorbed in many things; and his second method is obviously a modification of Ascham's plan of double translation.

In respect to *religious teaching*, he denounces the practice of using the Bible as a book for exercising and improving the talent of children in reading, a practice, which, I should hope, is quite extinct at the present day. Indeed, he looks with disfavour on the practice of using the Bible as a text-book at all.

'There are some parts of Scripture,' he says, 'which may be proper to be put into the hands of a child to engage him to read, such as are the story of Joseph and his brethren, of David and Goliath, of David and Jonathan, &c., and others that he should be made to read for his instruction, as that, "What you would have others do unto you, do you the same unto them," and such other easy and plain moral rules which, being fitly chosen, might often be made use of, both for reading and instruction together, and so often read till they are thoroughly fixed in the memory; and these afterwards, as he grows ripe for them, may in their turns, on fit occasions, be inculcated as the standing and sacred rules of his life and actions. But the reading of the whole Scripture indifferently, is what, I think, is very inconvenient for children, till after having been made acquainted with the plainest fundamental parts of it, they have got some kind of general view of what they ought principally to believe and practise.' (p. 240.)

He is accordingly in favour of a text-book, containing a summary of Bible history:—' To this purpose I conclude, it would be well if there were made a good history of the Bible for young people to read; wherein, if everything that is fit to be put into it, were laid down in its due order of time, and several things omitted, which are suited only to riper age, that confusion, which is usually produced by promiscuous reading of the Scripture as it lies now bound up in our Bibles, would be avoided.' (p. 298.)

These recommendations are very judicious, and are generally carried out in the Bible teaching pursued in most schools at the present day.

Locke's book contains suggestions on the learning of other branches of knowledge, but I have taken up those that are more immediately interesting to the elementary teacher, who, if he wish to pursue the subject further, may very profitably peruse the book for himself; and I now finish this chapter by quoting a few appropriate sentences from a Scotch philosopher, whose name has already appeared in these pages. 'It has often been remarked,' he says, 'that Locke's "Thoughts" display less originality than might have been expected from so bold and powerful a thinker; but it ought to be remembered that, on the most important points discussed in them, new suggestions are not now to be looked for, and that the great object of the reader should be, not to learn something which he never heard of before, but to learn among the multiplicity of discordant precepts current in the world, *which* of them were sanctioned, and *which* reprobated by the judgment of Locke. | The candid and unreserved thoughts of such a writer upon such subjects as education, and the culture of the intellectual powers, possess an intrinsic value which is not diminished by the consideration of their triteness. They not only serve to illustrate the peculiarities of the author's own character and views; but, considered in a practical light, come recommended to us by all the additional weight of his discriminating experience.'*

Locke's health, as I have stated before, was all through life very delicate, and required his constant care. Symptoms of the disease (asthma) of which he died appeared as early as 1671. During the last years of his life, increasing infirmities confined him to the retirement he had chosen at Oates, in Essex, where he occupied his time in literary occupations, congenial to his taste, chiefly in studying and in writing commentaries on St. Paul's Epistles. In 1704, his disorder greatly increased, and, on the 28th October, he died, as a Christian should die, happy in the consciousness of a well spent life, and yet more in the firm faith of the great truths of the Gospel.†

Locke's talents were of a versatile character, his writings on Money, on Trade, and on the principles of Government being equally well known with his works on Psychology and Education. Lord Campbell, in his "Lives of the Chancellors," styles him 'the author of the "Essay on the Human Understanding," the analyst of the Principles of Free Government, the apostle of Toleration, the first intelligent

* "Collected Works of Dugald Stewart," vol. I, p. 245.
† King's "Life of Locke," vol. II, p. 46.

advocate of useful Education, the founder of Free Trade in England.'*

From the following traits in his character, recorded by Lord King, the young teacher may derive two useful hints.

'He knew something of almost everything which can be useful to mankind, and was thoroughly master of all that he had studied; but he showed his superiority by not appearing to value himself in any way on account of his great attainments.

'He felt pleasure in conversing with all sorts of people, and tried to profit by their information, which arose not only from the good education he had received, but from the opinion he entertained, that there was nobody from whom something useful could not be got.'†

* Vol. VI, p. 69. † Vol. II, pp. 54, 55.

HENRY PESTALOZZI.

Early Life and Character—Studies first for the Church, then for the Law, at last decides on Farming—Marriage—Converts his Farm into an Industrial School—Result of the experiment—Takes to Writing Books on Education—Volunteers to teach the Orphans of Stanz—Invents the Simultaneous and Monitorial Systems—Object Lessons—Lessons on Form, Number, and Language—Arithmetic—On Teaching Geography—His Practice and his Theories—Influence of his Teaching on English Education—His Character.

EVERY young teacher is desirous to hear something of Pestalozzi, who is, without question, one of the most remarkable schoolmasters on record. Who has not heard of Pestalozzian schools, and Pestalozzian lessons, and in what comprehensive treatise on education does the name of Pestalozzi not appear? The young schoolmaster's curiosity on this subject should by all means be gratified, as Pestalozzi's life is one that is especially attractive to youthful minds, still fresh, ardent, and enthusiastic; and it presents a glorious example of self-sacrifice, of which, as it occurs within their own profession, teachers should be especially proud. It is a life which at the same time gives warning by its mistakes and failings, a life which stands forth as a beacon over the rocks on which Pestalozzi himself made shipwreck. Happily the beacon shines with a bright and clear light, for numerous books have been written about him, and he himself has left valuable information regarding his system in his own writings. Indeed, Pestalozzi's system and methods of teaching are best ascertained from his books, for it is generally acknowledged that he did more for education by his writings than by his personal work as a teacher. His personal work, however, is deeply interesting; but in reading an account of it the student should be prepared rather to hear a pleasant though somewhat sad story than to find the narrative full of professional hints. To the experienced teacher, likewise, the life may prove interesting; because, in studying it, he sees a workman struggling on without proper tools— observes the exercise of his own craft in its rudest beginnings.

Henry Pestalozzi was a Swiss, having been born at Zurich in 1746. His ancestors were of Italian extraction, who, being Protestants, were obliged, during the troubled period of the Reformation, to take refuge in Switzerland, and had chosen for their abode a city marked for its attachment to their faith.*

Pestalozzi had the misfortune to lose his father when he was only six years old, which deprived him of the usual fatherly and manly influences brought to bear on a boy's education. 'I was brought up,' he relates, 'by the best of mothers, like a spoiled child. I never left the domestic hearth from one year to another.'† He thus became, in every sense, a 'mother's child'—a term which appropriately pictures to us the affectionate, home-loving, sensitive, almost womanly nature of the man. The love thus imbibed from his mother's precepts and practice became a moving spring in his life; his veneration for mothers, and his regard for the domestic hearth, which shine so conspicuously in his works, may both be traced to its influence. The influence of a female servant, too, named Barbara, to whom Pestalozzi's father, with his dying breath, commended his widow and family, must not be forgotten. The fidelity and devotedness with which she discharged the office she undertook, and the frugality and prudence which she displayed throughout, impressed on the tender mind of

* " Memoir of Pestalozzi," by Dr. Mayo.
† Raumer's " Pestalozzi," translated by Tilleard, p. 1.

Pestalozzi that strong sense of the virtues of the lower orders, that respect and love for the poor, which marked his character, and exercised so powerful an influence on his life. Thus brought up, he saw the world only within the narrow limits of his mother's parlour, and within the equally narrow limits of his schoolroom, being almost a stranger to the human life of the world around him. It is not to be wondered at, therefore, that his character was deficient in many qualities which are necessary for success in life. Intensely human and humane, sympathetic and benevolent, he was at the same time singularly unpractical and indiscreet, and deficient in calm circumspection and foresight. An anecdote is related which portrays this indiscretion in an almost amusing light. In the darkest period of his career, when his family was without the necessaries of life, he went to a friend's house to borrow a little money; and on his return, chancing to meet a peasant, who was bewailing the loss of a cow, Pestalozzi thrust the borrowed money into the poor man's hand, and ran off to escape his thanks. Testimony to the same effect is afforded by a remark of Lavater's—one of Pestalozzi's most intimate friends. 'If I were a prince,' he said, 'I would consult Pestalozzi in everything that concerns the people and the improvement of their condition, but I would never trust him with a farthing of money.' (Raumer, p. 16.)

Pestalozzi received a tolerable education, in a country celebrated for the facility of attaining it. Of his school days he relates, that in all boys' games he was clumsy and helpless; his playmates, who saw only the outside of the boy, nicknaming him 'Harry Oddity, of Foolstown.' While he generally seized with quickness and accuracy on the essential matter of the various subjects of instruction, he was very generally indifferent and thoughtless as to the forms in which it was given. At the same time, while he was behind his fellows in some parts of a subject, in other parts he often surpassed them in an unusual degree. He also frankly confesses that his mind had a liking for many branches of knowledge, while he neglected the means of acquiring them, or acquiring them in a sufficiently accurate way—traits which foreshadowed his subsequent career.

From his maternal grandfather, who was pastor of a country village, and with whom he used to reside several months every year, Pestalozzi received deep and lasting religious impressions, and also an inclination for the clerical profession, to which his thoughts were in the first instance directed. But his want of accuracy and characteristic carelessness interfered with this intention. He broke down more than once in his trial sermon, was unable to repeat even the Lord's Prayer correctly, and thus fell into the list of 'stickit' ministers. Undaunted by this failure, he took to the study of law, towards which he was strongly drawn by his innate 'hate of wrong and love of right'; for Switzerland was at this time suffering from internal dissensions, arising both from religious and political causes, the sight of which profoundly affected Pestalozzi's mind, and made him anxious to devote his life to their amelioration. Indeed, from his earliest years, in common with his schoolmates, he had had an irresistible desire to do great deeds for his unhappy country, and was induced by his teachers to keep before his mind the watchwords of 'Independence, freedom, self-sacrifice, and patriotism'; and we are not unprepared to find that, when only a lad of fifteen, he had joined an association of youthful enthusiasts, founded by Lavater, which had for its object the impeachment of unworthy governors and ministers of religion. Fired with visionary ideas, Pestalozzi believed that the study of law would afford him, sooner or later, opportunities of exercising an active influence on the civil condition of his native town, and even of his native land. But, alas! for the young man's ambition, excitement and hard study told upon his health, and he became dangerously ill. His doctor advised him to give up his pursuits for a time, and to seek recreation in the country. He followed the advice most literally, burnt his manuscripts, and betook himself to farming. The person, under whom he placed himself for agricultural training, was a man of skill and ingenuity, who had devised a plan of his own for the successful cultivation of madder, which was at that moment attracting public attention. Before he had been many months under training, Pestalozzi, with characteristic haste and inexperience, conceived the project of carrying out experiments upon madder on his own account; and, with this object in view, he induced a rich commercial firm in Zurich to join him in purchasing a hundred acres of barren heath land, near the village of Birr. On this ground Pestalozzi ordered a handsome house to be built, giving the whole estate the name of Neuhof (New Farm). This was in 1767, when he was twenty-one years of age; and we are not surprised to know that he was then passing through a common phase of youthful experience. He was in love, and with the daughter of a wealthy merchant in Zurich. To this lady (Anna Schulthess) he wrote a letter (one of some hundreds, we may be sure), which has been fortunate enough to secure attention from every biographer. To do it justice, it is a noteworthy production, as it gives considerable insight into the workings of his heart, and even affords a glimpse into his future life. The following are a few of the most remarkable passages :—

'My dear and only friend, those of my faults, which appear to me most important in relation to the situation in which I may be placed in afterlife, are, improvidence, incautiousness, and a want of presence of mind to meet unexpected changes in my prospects. I know not how far these failings may be diminished by my efforts to counteract them by calm judgment and experience. At present, I have them still in such a degree that I dare not conceal them from the maiden I love ; they are faults, my dear, which deserve your fullest consideration. I have *other* faults, arising from my irritability and sensitiveness, which oftentimes will not submit to my judgment. I very frequently allow myself to run into excesses in praising and blaming, in my likings and dislikings ; I cleave so strongly to many things which I possess, that the force with which I feel myself attached to them often exceeds the bounds of reason. Whenever my country or my friend is unhappy, I am myself unhappy. Direct your attention to this weakness. There will be times when the cheerfulness and tranquillity of my soul will suffer under it. If even it does not hinder me in the discharge of my duties, yet I shall scarcely ever be great enough to fulfil them in such adverse circumstances with the cheerfulness and tranquillity of a wise man who is ever true to himself. Of my great and, indeed, very reprehensible negligence in all matters of etiquette, and generally in all matters which are not in themselves of importance, I need not speak; any one may see them at first sight of me. I also owe you the open confession, my dear, that I shall always consider my duties towards my beloved partner subordinate to my duties towards my country; and that, although I shall be the tenderest husband, nevertheless I hold myself bound to be inexorable to the tears of my wife if she should ever attempt to restrain me by them from the direct performance of my duties as a citizen, whatever this might lead to. My wife shall be the confidante of my heart, the partner of all my secret counsels. A great and honest simplicity shall reign in my house. And one thing more. My life will not pass without important and very critical undertakings. I shall not forget the precepts of Menalk, and my first resolutions to devote myself wholly to my country. I shall never, from fear of man, refrain from speaking when I see that the good of my country calls upon me to speak. My whole heart is my country's. I will risk all to alleviate the need and misery of my fellow-countrymen. What consequences may the undertakings to which I feel myself urged on draw after them! how unequal to them am I! and how imperative is my duty to shew you the possibility of the great dangers which they may bring upon me.' (Raumer, pp. 6, 7.) The young lady, beautiful and rich as she was (while Pestalozzi was neither), proved worthy of his trust. They were married in 1769, and till the date of her death in 1815, she continued to prove, in the language of Scripture, a 'helpmeet' to him. It was not long, however, till troubles came upon the youthful couple. Pestalozzi's attempt to cultivate madder proved a failure, solely, as he himself confesses, on account of his incapacity for every kind of undertaking which required practical wisdom and tact. The Zurich firm became alarmed, and withdrew its money. Thus left to his own resources, he conceived the idea of converting his farm into a model industrial school for poor children, one of the boldest undertakings in the annals of private life.[*] The idea of such a school is now familiar to us; it was then

[*] Biber's " Pestalozzi," p. 14.

new. The proposal met with approval from many philanthropic and influential persons, and the school was opened in 1775. Before long there were fifty pupils in attendance, literally gathered from the highways. In summer, the children were chiefly employed in field work; in winter, in spinning, and other handicrafts—Pestalozzi meanwhile carrying on their education. Now was realized in part his youthful dream of improving the condition of the poor. Brought into immediate contact with these wretched paupers, he strove to train them to habits of industry, as well as to give them instruction. For five long years he devoted his whole time and energy to this work, endeavouring to teach these children that, while labour was their lot and their duty, their first and most important employment, intellectual pursuits might be the privilege of their leisure hours. It was a noble and Christian-minded attempt, and we honour the hero who conceived and carried it out; but we need not wonder that it failed for want of funds. The children in many cases behaved badly, running away, in several instances, as soon as they had been provided with a suit of clothes. 'Before I was aware of it,' says Pestalozzi, 'I was deeply involved in debt, and the greater part of my dear wife's property and expectations had in an instant, as it were, gone up in smoke.' In a letter to a friend, written twenty years afterwards, he gives the following interesting account of his experiences:—' I lived for years together in a circle of more than fifty pauper children; in poverty did I share my bread with them, and lived myself like a pauper, to try if I could teach paupers to live as men. The plan which I had formed for their education embraced agriculture, manufacture, and commerce. In no one of the three departments did I possess any practical ability for the management of details, nor was my mind of a cast to keep up persevering attention to little things; and in an insulated position, with limited means, I was unable to procure such assistance as might have made up for my own deficiencies. In a short time I was surrounded with embarrassments, and saw the great object of my wishes defeated. In the struggle, however, in which this attempt involved me, I had learned a vast deal of truth, and I was never more fully convinced of the importance of my views and plans than at the moment when they seemed to be for ever set at rest by a total failure.'

Pestalozzi's labours were not lost. More than a hundred children were rescued from ignorance and degradation; and Pestalozzi was supplied with a rich store of experience, that was of the greatest service to him in his future plans and operations. His attempt also suggested to others the idea of starting similar institutions, both on the Continent and in this country. It was Pestalozzi's school that suggested to De Fellenberg the one which he established on his estate of Hofwyl, near Berne, and which, under skilful management, succeeded in realizing Pestalozzi's idea. His grateful countrymen could not have raised any memorial to him more appropriate than the Orphan School which they founded at Olsberg, in Aargau, after the celebration of his centenary birthday in 1846. If such establishments are, even at the present day, not successful in a pecuniary point of view, and require State aid and voluntary contributions, it should make us judge more leniently the failure of the man who grappled with the difficulties of the task for the first time.

In 1780, Pestalozzi was obliged to break up the establishment at Neuhof. His situation was distressing; his family, as related in the foregoing anecdote, were on the point of starvation; his wife fell into a severe and tedious illness, during which shall we imagine that she pondered over the substance of the famous love-letter, and wept? His friends, at all events, declared that he was a lost man, and that nothing further could be done

HIS FIRST PUBLICATION.

for him. For eighteen years after,* he did not engage in any educational undertaking—eighteen gloomy years, during which he struggled with difficulties without, and with doubt and despondency within. 'My head was grey,' he exclaims, 'but I was still a child.' And his child-like nature found scope in writing down his ideas in books; and it is from them, as I have said, more than from his personal teaching, that we judge of him as an educationist. His first publication was called "The Evening Hour of a Hermit," a series of educational aphorisms, very similar in its scope to the "Didactica Magna" of Comenius, and in the calm thoughts of which there is no trace of the disturbed state of the author's mind. The following is a brief, yet sufficiently distinctive, extract:—

'What man is, what he needs, what elevates him and degrades him, what strengthens him and weakens him,—such is the knowledge needed both by shepherds of the people and by the inmate of the most lowly hut.

'Everywhere humanity feels this want. Everywhere it struggles to satisfy it with labour and earnestness. For the want of it men live restless

---

* See Morf's "Zur Biographie Pestalozzi's" for many touching passages from diaries and letters, shewing the inner life of the man during this painful period.

lives, and at death they cry aloud that they have not fulfilled the purposes of their being. Their end is not the ripening of the perfect fruits of the year, which, in full completion, are laid away for the repose of the winter. . . .

'The powers of conferring blessings on humanity are not a gift of art or of accident. They exist with their fundamental principles in the inmost nature of all men. Their development is the universal need of humanity.

'Central point of life, individual destiny of man, thou art the book of *nature*. In thee lieth the power and the plan of that wise teacher; and every school education not erected upon the principles of human development leads astray.

'The happy infant learns by this road what his mother is to him; and thus grows within him the actual sentiment of love and gratitude, before he can understand the words duty or thanks. . . . The truth which rises from our inmost being is universal human truth, and would serve as a truth for the reconciliation of those who are quarrelling by thousands over its husks.

'Man, it is thyself, the inner consciousness of thy powers, which is the object of the education of nature.

'The general elevation of these inward powers of the human mind, to a pure human wisdom, is the universal purpose of the education even of the lowest man. The practice, application, and use of these powers and this wisdom under special circumstances and conditions of humanity, is education for a professional or social condition. These must always be kept subordinate to the general object of human training. . . . Nature develops all the human faculties by practice, and their growth depends upon their exercise. . . . Men, fathers, force not the faculties of your children into paths too distant, before they have attained strength by exercise, and avoid harshness and over fatigue. . . . You leave the right order when, before making them sensitive to truth and wisdom by the real knowledge of actual objects, you engage them in the thousand-fold confusions of word learning and opinions, and lay the foundation of their mental character, and of the first determination of their powers, not with truth and actual obligations, but with sounds, and speech, and words. . . . And the source of justice and of all blessing for the world, the source of love and brotherly feeling among men, rests on the great thought of religion that we are children of God, and that belief of this truth is the sure ground of all blessing for the world. . . . That men have lost the disposition of children towards God is the greatest misfortune of the world, inasmuch as it renders impossible all God's fatherly education of them; and the restoring of this lost childlike disposition is the redemption of the lost children of God upon earth.'*

The "Evening Hour" may be likened to the rough draft of the architect, or, to take a different simile, it is the outline or skeleton round whose bones Pestalozzi strove to create living flesh and blood, in his future writings and imperfect practice. Each aphorism is a text for a discourse, and his life is, as it were, a series of attempts to put his own preaching into practice. To this educational programme he appealed many years afterwards to prove that he had always held the views which he struggled to realise.

In 1781 was published "Leonard and Gertrude," the book on which his fame as an author chiefly rests. It is an educational novel, containing an admirable picture of village life in Switzerland, and is perhaps his greatest work, as it is certainly the one that has had the widest circulation and influence. The principal character in the story is Gertrude, whose manner of keeping her house and training her children is Pestalozzi's ideal, and is intended as a model for all housekeepers and mothers. Gertrude is consulted even in the

* "Educational Reformers," pp. 310, 311; Morf, p. 320.

management of the village school, the re-organization of which forms one of the chief matters of interest. The following picture is given of the schoolmaster, Gluelphi by name, who bases his system of discipline on the practice of Gertrude in the domestic circle.

'Gluelphi was deeply impressed with the truth that education is not imparted by *words* but by *facts*. For kindling the flame of love and devotion in their souls, he trusted not to the hearing and learning by heart of passages setting forth the beauties of love and its blessings, but he endeavoured to manifest to them a spirit of genuine charity, and to encourage them to the practice of it, both by example and precept. He led them to live in love. He presented to their minds the distresses and sufferings of others—not of men who had lived thousands of years before them, and at thousands of miles' distance, but of those who were near them—whose tears they saw flowing—in whose emaciated countenances they could themselves read the inscription of hunger—whose nakedness and helplessness made an immediate appeal to their senses. By the sight of misery, he endeavoured to excite commiseration in the hearts of the children, and to lead them to reflect on the causes of distress and suffering, and on the means of alleviating them. He rendered them attentive to the afflictions of their fellow-creatures. If there was any one ill in the house of any of the children, were it father or mother, or brother or sister, or even the meanest servant, he never failed to ask the child the moment he entered the schoolroom, how the invalid did, and the child had to give a detailed and accurate account. Gluelphi did not take half answers on these occasions, but was so particular in his inquiries that, if the child had not asked the sick person at home, he would at once betray his ignorance, and be overwhelmed with such confusion that he would certainly never leave home again, without having informed himself on the subject. The children were asked likewise, whether they had spoken themselves to the invalid, and whether they had contributed to alleviate his sufferings, if it were only by avoiding every noise and bustle in the house. Nor did he ever omit the question, "Are you praying every morning and every evening for your invalid, that God may restore him to health?"' (Biber, p. 142.)

Pestalozzi says that his object in writing "Leonard and Gertrude," which flowed from his pen he knew not how, was to bring about a better education of the people, based on proper principles. His heart bled at the sight of their ignorance and misery; and looking around in vain for a staff of schoolmasters who would teach after his manner and in his spirit, and deploring the want of institutions where such teachers could be trained, he conceived the noble idea of shewing how every mother might be the teacher and the trainer of her own family. 'Eureka!' he cried in the exultation of his heart, 'I will place the education of the people in the hands of the mothers; I will transplant it out of the school-room into the parlour.' Gertrude was created as a model mother, and all mothers were to seek to be like her. But how was this to be effected? How were the mothers in the lower classes to be qualified for instructing? Pestalozzi anticipated this difficulty by drawing up a series of compendiums for mothers, by following which they were to be qualified for teaching their children. They had only to keep strictly to these books in the work of instruction; and if they did this, the mother of the most limited capacity would be found to instruct just as well as the most talented. Grand as this scheme of universal instruction by mothers undoubtedly was, we regret to find that Pestalozzi's compendiums were most unsuitable for the purpose in view. His principle, that a child should begin to learn, first of all, what lies nearest to him, led him to the idea that no natural object lay nearer to a child than its own body, and that therefore it should begin by observing that. The "Book for Mothers" accordingly describes the human frame, with all its limbs and parts of limbs, down to the minutest joints; and the mother is to go through the book, word for word, calling the child's attention constantly to the parts of its own body. Who, after this, can question the source from which Jacotot drew one of his most famous paradoxes? "Anybody can teach, and, moreover, he can teach that which he does not know." Fancy what a gabbling of anatomical and physiological terms there would be, day by day, in this large city of ours, with its half a million of inhabitants, if Pestalozzi's compendiums had met with general adoption! Ludicrous as the thought may be, we must not forget that this idea of his, the home instruction by mothers, is one which every successful teacher takes advantage of; and in the mutual co-operation of teachers and parents in the preparation of lessons we have the happiest and best results. The schoolmaster, to borrow a remark of Dr. Wiese's, in his "Letters on English Education," shews them *the way to learn;* at home they put the precept into practice.

Equally inappropriate are the lessons on sound

which Pestalozzi recommends the mother to give to her children. 'The spelling-book,' he says, 'should contain the entire range of sounds of which the language consists, and portions of it should be repeated daily in every family, not only by the child that is going through the exercises to learn how to spell, but also by mothers within hearing of the child in the cradle, in order that these sounds may, by frequent repetition, be so deeply impressed on the memory of the child, even while it is yet unable to pronounce any one of them, that they shall never be forgotten. No one imagines to what a degree the attention of infants is aroused by the repetition of such simple sounds as ba, ba, ba ; da, da, da ; ma, ma, ma ; la, la, la ; &c., or what a charm such repetition has for them.'

'Such lessons,' says Raumer, 'are enough to scare away the child's guardian angels.'

But however mistaken the suggestions of Pestalozzi are, there is, no doubt, truth in his opinion that education should begin from the cradle ; and, fortunately, as Herbert Spencer observes, 'the ordinary practice of the nursery educates the child to some extent, though much remains to be done.'*

Pestalozzi published other works of an educa-

* " Education," p. 82.

tional and philosophical character which it is unnecessary to notice here, and it was fortunate that his enthusiasm and energy were called into renewed action of an educational character by events that arose out of the French Revolution. The sound of war broke forth, and awoke him from his literary dreams. A new epoch was at hand for Switzerland, which the French invaders elevated into a republic, christening it 'New Helvetia.' Pestalozzi declared himself in favour of the new order of things, and his pen was engaged by the Directors. The result was not favourable to his social advancement. He wrote in favour of education as a means of elevating the people. The Directors had no knowledge of the people, and, caring nothing for their improvement, found that he was not the man for them. Fortunately a piece of service presented itself of a congenial nature, which restored Pestalozzi to himself. The Roman Catholic canton of Unterwalden, the land of William Tell, having refused to acknowledge the new constitution, was invaded by the French, and its capital, Stanz, was pillaged and burnt. A cry of grief arose from its widows and orphan children, and the Swiss members of the Directory, lamenting the calamity, hastened to do something which might mitigate the impression which the news of the event could not fail to produce throughout the land. They proposed to Pestalozzi that he should proceed to Stanz, and take charge of the orphan and destitute children. His heart leaped at the thought. Now was there an opportunity afforded him of making an experiment of his plan of national education. 'I went,' he writes; 'I would have gone into the remotest cleft of the mountains to come nearer my aim, and now I really did come nearer.'

But imagine his position. The school-room set apart for him was the only habitable apartment of an unfinished convent. Children, to the number of eighty, came flocking in, many of them orphans, and these ate and slept in school. Apparatus, books, there were none. What could he do? Let my readers close their eyes and reflect what they would have done in the circumstances. What Pestalozzi did will be best described in his own words :—

'Alone, destitute of all means of instruction, and of all other assistance, I united in my person the offices of superintendent, paymaster, steward, and sometimes chambermaid in a half-ruined house. I was surrounded with ignorance, disease, and with every kind of novelty. The number of children rose by degrees; all of different ages; some full of pretensions; others trained to open beggary; and all, with a few solitary exceptions, entirely ignorant. What a task! to educate, to develop these children! What a task! I ventured upon it. I stood in the midst of them, pronouncing various sounds, and asking the children to imitate them. Whoever saw it was struck with the effect. Being obliged to instruct the children by myself, without any assistance, I learnt the art of teaching a great number together; and, as I had no other means of bringing the instruction before them, than that of pronouncing everything to them loudly and distinctly, I was naturally led to the idea of making them draw, write, and work all at the same time. The confusion of so many voices repeating my words, suggested the necessity of keeping time in our exercises, and I soon found that this contributed materially to make their impressions stronger and more distinct. Their total ignorance forced me to dwell a long time on the simplest elements, and I was thus led to perceive how much higher a degree of interest and power is obtained by persevering attention to the elementary parts, until they be perfectly familiar to the mind; and what confidence and interest the child is inspired with, by the consciousness of complete and perfect attainment, even in the lowest stage of instruction. Never before had I so deeply felt the important bearing, which the first elements of every branch of knowledge have upon its complete outline, and what immense deficiencies in the final result of education must arise from the confusion and imperfections of the simplest beginnings. To bring these to maturity and perfection in the child's mind became, now, a main object of my attention; and the success far surpassed my expectations. The consciousness of energies hitherto unknown to themselves was rapidly developed in the children, and a general sense of order and harmony began to prevail among them. They felt their own power, and the tediousness of the common school vanished like a spectre from the room. They were determined to try; they succeeded; they persevered; they accomplished, and were delighted. Their mood was not that of laborious learning, it was the joy of unknown powers aroused from sleep; their hearts and minds were elevated by the anticipation of what these powers would enable them to attempt and to effect.'*

* The remarks in the above extract, in reference to the advantage of dwelling upon the elements, are so cogent, that they attracted the attention of Dr. Gordon, H.M. Inspector of Schools, before whom I read a lecture on Pestalozzi in 1868, and from his notice of them in his report to the Committee of Council, they attracted the attention of their Lordships, who, in their general report of the same year, refer to them in support of their system of examination contained in the Revised Code. See "Blue Book," 1868-1869, pp. xxv, 476.

This extract is from a well known book of his entitled, " How Gertrude Teaches her Children." Observe his adoption of the simultaneous system, which had been made use of in the Austrian schools before his time, and on which his panegyrist, Dr. Biber, passes enthusiastic eulogy, at the same time observing that it should be a rule with the teacher never to employ this means for bringing a *new* subject before his pupils; but to confine its use exclusively to revision; and adding that the simultaneous repetition, whether in a musical form or not, of addition, multiplication, pence, weight, and other tables, so common in public charity schools, far from forming a part of Pestalozzi's plan, is, on the contrary, a mere caricature of it.

In another passage from " How Gertrude Teaches her Children," we observe that Pestalozzi also introduced at Stanz the monitorial system, which, though quite original on his part, is as old as Comenius. 'Children became the teachers of children. They endeavoured to carry into effect what I proposed; and in doing so, they themselves frequently traced the means of execution. Their spontaneous activity was called out in every direction, as far as the elements of knowledge go; and I was brought to the firm conviction, that all instruction, to have a truly

THE MONITORIAL SYSTEM. 79

enlightening and cultivating influence, *must be drawn out of the children* (Stow), and, as it were, begotten within their minds. To this, also, I was brought chiefly by necessity. Seeing that I had no assistant teachers, I placed a child of superior capacities between two of inferior powers. He threw his arms round their necks; he taught them what he knew, and they learned from him what they knew not. They sat by the side of each other with heart-felt affection. Joy and love animated their souls; the life which was awakened within them, and which had taken hold of their minds, carried both teachers and learners forward with a rapidity and cheerfulness which this process of mutual enlivening alone could produce.' (Biber, p. 169.)

In connection with this extract, Biber notices a misunderstanding which had gone forth on the subject of Pestalozzi's method, to the effect that his mutual system is the same as that of Bell and Lancaster.

'Pestalozzi employed one child to teach another. This is mutual instruction, no doubt. Bell and Lancaster employed one child to teach another: this, too, is mutual instruction; but Pestalozzi awakened in one child a consciousness of his powers and a tendency to mental self-activity; and the child so awakened he called in to assist him in awakening other children in the same manner and by the same means. Pestalozzi led his children by the love which they bore him, by the moral ascendency which he had gained over them; so that, whithersoever he led the way, they were willing to follow; and in the same manner he taught his children to treat one another. Bell and Lancaster, on the contrary, drill one child through an artificial machinery of lifeless tasks, and the child so drilled they employ to drill others in the same manner and by the same means. Bell and Lancaster restrain their children by fear, and excite them by artificial and mercenary motives, that for hire's sake the natures of the children may yield themselves to the unnature of the system; and the same means of direct and indirect compulsion they place in the hands of their subordinate drillers.' (p. 170.)

Pestalozzi was unwearied, also, in inculcating moral lessons to these neglected children. He strove to promote mutual kindness and good feeling among them, and to train them to the practice of love and charity. Thus, when Altorf, in a neighbouring canton, was laid in ashes, he informed them of the event, and suggested that they should receive some of the suffering children into their own asylum. 'Hundreds of children,' he told them, 'are now wandering about as you were last year, without a home, perhaps without food or clothing.' 'Oh yes, do send for them to come here,' they all cried. Pestalozzi reminded them that such a step would entail additional privations on themselves; they should have to share their bedding and their clothing with them, and eat less and work more than before. 'Never mind,' they cried; 'though we should be less well-off ourselves, we should be very glad to have those poor children amongst us.' (p. 37.)

'In the midst of his children,' says Biber, 'he forgot that there was any world besides the asylum. And as their circle was a universe to him, so he was to them all in all. From morning to night he was the centre of their existence. To him they owed every comfort and every enjoyment; and whatever hardships they had to endure, he was their fellow-sufferer. He partook of their meals, and slept among them. In the evening he prayed with them, and from his conversation they dropped into the arms of slumber. At the first dawn of day it was his voice that called them to the light of the rising sun and to the praise of their Heavenly Father. All day he stood amongst them, teaching the ignorant and assisting the helpless, encouraging the weak and admonishing the transgressor. His hand was daily with them joined in theirs; his eye, beaming with benevolence, rested on them. He wept when they wept, and rejoiced when they rejoiced. He was to them a father, and they were to him as children.'

Another noteworthy feature of his teaching at Stanz was the giving of object lessons, of which he is the real originator. But these lessons were of the rudest kind, their style being pretty nearly the following. Suppose the lesson for the day had been on a piece of sponge, Pestalozzi, holding up the specimen before the children, would sing out in a high monotone, 'This is sponge,' requiring them to repeat the sentence three times simultaneously. Then he would proceed, 'Sponge is an animal product.' 'Sponge is amorphous.' 'Sponge is porous.' 'Sponge is absorbent.' And so on in the same manner. Such lessons were obviously not calculated to train the observing powers of the children, but were rather, like the majority of Pestalozzi's lessons, lessons in language merely. Words, and not things or facts in science, were all that the children could pick up and take away, if indeed they did carry away anything at all. The cause of this failure in carrying out his own ideal is not far to seek. Pestalozzi himself reveals it with the utmost candour. 'I never pretended to teach any art or science,' he says; 'in fact, there is not one with which I am myself acquainted.'

Pestalozzi's idea, however, was caught up by his disciples, and in a great measure realized. To Dr. Mayo belongs the credit of introducing object lessons successfully into England, and his "Lessons on Objects," now in the twentieth edition, was the forerunner of a class of school books which have been brought to much excellence, in proof of which I need only name such manuals as Ross's "How to Train Young Eyes and Ears," Lake's "Object Lessons," Walker's "Object Lessons," and Calkin's "New Primary Object Lessons" (an American book), of which I have had personal experience. That even with these valuable aids, the giving of object lessons is not properly understood, may be inferred from the following remarks on them by the late Professor Moseley, H.M. Inspector of Schools :—

'A teacher proposing to give an oral lesson on coal, for instance, holds a piece of it up before his class, and having secured their attention, he probably asks them to which kingdom it belongs—animal, vegetable, or mineral—a question in no case of much importance, and to be answered, in the case of coal, doubtfully. Having, however, extracted that answer which he intends to get from the children, he induces them by many ingenious devices, much circumlocution, and an extravagant expenditure of the time of the school, to say that it is a *solid*, that it is *heavy*, that it is *opaque*, that it is *black*, that it is *friable*, and that it is *combustible*. And then the time has probably expired, and the lesson on the science of common things, assumed to be so useful to a child, is completed.

'In such a lesson, the teacher affords evidence of no other knowledge of the particular thing that was the subject of it, than the children might be supposed to have known before the lesson began. He gives it easily, because the form is the same for every lesson; the blanks having only to be differently filled up every time it is repeated. All that it is adapted for is to teach them the meanings of some unusual words—words useless to them, because they apply to abstract ideas, and which, as the type of all such lessons is the same, he has probably often taught them before.

'He has shewn some knowledge of words, but none of things. Of the particular thing called coal, as distinguished from any other thing, he knows nothing more than the child; but only of certain properties common to it, and almost everything else, and of certain words useless to poor children, which describe those properties : coal is a *common* thing to a child, one with which its daily observation is familiar, intimately connected with the uses of its life—a substance about which it might be taught many things which would probably be of great use to it in after life—things which it would not be likely ever to know, unless it were so taught them. But they are not *these* things; and if the science of common things is to be so taught, as to be of any future use to the child, it must not be this science.'*

'It may be proper to remark that the original Pestalozzian object lessons are not fairly chargeable with the folly of teaching children long adjectives of foreign extraction, as the names of the qualities of the objects. This is an additional error, into which English teachers have been led by the mixed character of our language. In the German, which is a primitive language, the words denoting the qualities of the objects are either simple words in the language, or are formed from such, and are therefore readily understood by the German children.' (Tilleard, p. 56.)

Pestalozzi divided his own object lessons into three classes. (1) Those on Form ; (2) on Number ; (3) on Speech ; and as we learn from

* " Minutes of Council," 1853.

perusing "How Gertrude teaches her Children," his great object in giving these lessons was to cultivate the observing powers of the children from the earliest stage of education, a principle on which he seems to hold quite as clear views as our latest educationist, Herbert Spencer; indeed, the latter goes the length of stating that, "the realization of the Pestalozzian idea remains to be achieved." The following is an interesting extract from the book referred to.

'Whatever man may attempt to do by his tuition, he can, at best, do no more than assist the child's nature in the effort which it makes for its own development; and to do this, so that the impression made upon the child may always be commensurate to, and in harmony with, the measure and character of the powers already unfolded in him, is the great secret of education. The perceptions to which the child is to be led by his instructor must therefore necessarily be subjected to a certain order of succession, the beginning of which must be adapted to the very first unfolding of the child's powers, and its progress kept exactly parallel with that of the child's own development.

'This much I saw clearly, that the child may be brought to a high degree of knowledge, both of things and of language, before it would be rational to teach him reading or even spelling; and seeing this, I felt the necessity of leading children from their earliest infancy to a rational view of all things by presenting them in a manner calculated to draw forth the action of the different faculties upon every object. . . . Experience confirmed me in this notion! A mother, full of interest for the education of her child, entrusted me with the instruction of her little boy, then hardly three years of age. I saw him for some time, an hour every day; and with him too, I was merely, as it were, feeling the pulse of the method. I tried to convert letters, figures, and whatever else was at hand, into means of instruction; that is to say, I led him to form, concerning every object, distinct notions, and to express these notions clearly in language. I made him state positively what he knew of every object, its colour, its parts, its position, its shape, its number. Very soon I was obliged to lay aside the alphabet, that first torment of youth; he felt no interest in these dead signs; he would have nothing but things, or pictures of things; and in a short time he was enabled to express himself distinctly respecting any objects within the sphere of his knowledge. He gathered general information from the street, from the garden, and from the house, and upon the basis of clear and self-acquired notions, he soon learned to pronounce correctly even the most difficult names of plants and animals.' (Biber, p. 174.)

The knowledge thus acquired by the child from his own experience was styled by Pestalozzi intuitive knowledge; and perceiving the difficulty of getting teachers to carry on this system of lessons without help, he proceeded to draw up a series of text books on the subject, by following which they should be enabled to produce the results desired, a mistake similar to that which he made in drawing up the "Mother's Manual." In both experiments he quite justified the remark made to himself, by a member of the Executive Council of Berne, '*Vous voulez mécaniser l'education.*'

Pestalozzi taught in Stanz from September 1798, till June of the following year, his labours being brought to a close by the entry of French troops into the town, and their taking possession of the convent for the purposes of an hospital. He let the children return to their friends, and went into the Bernese Oberland to recruit his exhausted strength, and where, on reflecting on the ordeal he had just gone through, he was led to exclaim, 'It is a wonder I am still alive.' In the course of the year he returned, quite recruited in health, and obtained leave to teach in the elementary schools of Burgdorf, in the Canton Berne. In a short time the head master became jealous of him, and injurious reports were circulated in reference to his capacity. 'It was whispered,' he tells us, 'that I could not write, nor work accounts, nor even read properly,' and he adds, with amusing ingenuousness, 'popular reports are not always entirely devoid of truth ; it *is* true that I could not write, nor read, nor work accounts well.'

The following account of his teaching in Burgdorf, by one of his pupils, named Ramsauer, is not altogether favourable :—

'I got about as much regular schooling as the other scholars—namely, none at all; but his (Pestalozzi's) sacred zeal, his devoted love, which caused him to be entirely unmindful of himself; his serious and depressed state of mind, which struck even the children, made the deepest impression on me, and knit my child-like and grateful heart to his for ever.

'Pestalozzi's intention was that all the instruction given in this school should start from form, number, and language, and should have a constant reference to these elements. There was no regular plan in existence, neither was there a timetable, for which reason Pestalozzi did not tie himself down to any particular hours; but generally went on with the same subject for two or three hours together. There were about sixty of us, boys and girls, of ages varying from eight to fifteen years; the school hours were from eight till eleven in the morning, and from two to four in the afternoon. The instruction which we received was entirely limited to drawing, ciphering, and exercises in language. We neither read nor wrote, and accordingly we had neither reading nor writing books, nor were we required to commit to memory anything secular or sacred.

'For the drawing, we had neither copies to draw from nor directions what to draw; but only crayons and boards; and we were told to draw what we liked during the time that Pestalozzi was reading aloud sentences about natural history (as exercises in language). But we did not know what to draw, and so it happened that some drew men and women, some houses, and others strings, knots, and arabesques, or whatever else came into their heads. Pestalozzi never looked to see *what* we had drawn, or rather scribbled; but the clothes of all the scholars, especially the sleeves and elbows, gave unmistakeable evidence that they had been making due use of their crayons.

'For the ciphering, we had between every two scholars a small table pasted on millboard, on which in quadrangular fields were marked dots, which we had to count, to add together, to subtract, to multiply and divide by one another. It was out of these exercises that Krüsi and Buss constructed, first, the unity table, and afterwards the fraction tables. But, as Pestalozzi only allowed the scholars to go over and to repeat the exercises in their turns, and never questioned them nor set them tasks, these exercises, which were otherwise very good, remained without any great utility. He had not sufficient patience to allow things to be gone over again, or to put questions; and in his enormous zeal for the instruction of the whole school, he seemed not to concern himself in the slightest degree for the individual scholar.

'The best things we had with him were the exercises in language, at least those which he gave us on the paper-hangings of the school-room, which were real exercises in observation. These hangings were very old and a good deal torn, and before these we had frequently to stand for two or three hours together, and say what we observed in respect to the form, number, position, and colour of the figures painted on them, and the holes torn in them, and to express what we observed in sentences gradually increasing in length. On such occasions, he would say, "Boys, what do you see?" (He never named the girls.)

'*Answer.*—A hole (or rent) in the wainscot.
Pestalozzi.—Very good. Now repeat after me—
I see a hole in the wainscot.
I see a long hole in the wainscot.
Through the hole I see the wall.
Through the long narrow hole I see the wall.
Pestalozzi.—Repeat after me :—
I see figures on the paper hangings.
I see black figures on the paper hangings.
I see round black figures on the paper hangings.
I see a square yellow figure on the paper hangings.
Beside the square yellow figure, I see a black round figure.
The square figure is joined to the round one by a thick black stroke.

'And so on.
'Of less utility were those exercises in language which he took from natural history, and in which we had to repeat after him, and at the same time to draw, as I have already mentioned. He would say—

'Amphibious Animals—Crawling amphibious animals.
                              Creeping amphibious animals.
    Monkeys—   Long-tailed monkeys.
                            Short-tailed monkeys.

'And so on.
'We did not understand a word of this, for not a word was explained, and it was all spoken in

sing-song tone, and so rapidly and indistinctly, that it would have been a wonder if any one had understood anything of it, and had learnt anything from it; besides, Pestalozzi cried out so dreadfully loud and so continuously, that he could not hear us repeat after him, the less so as he never waited for us when he had read out a sentence, but went on without intermission, and read off a whole page at once. What he had thus read out was drawn up on a half-sheet of large-sized millboard, and our repetition consisted for the most part in saying the last word or syllable of each phrase, thus, "monkeys, monkeys"; or "keys, keys." There was never any questioning or recapitulation.' (Raumer, p. 36.) (How would this satisfy H.M. Inspectors?)

Imperfect as is the mode of teaching drawing related by Ramsauer, there is no doubt, from the following extract from a letter of Pestalozzi's, that he was fully alive to the educational value of the subject.

'A person who is in the habit of drawing, especially from nature, will easily perceive many circumstances which are commonly overlooked, and will form a much more correct impression, even of such objects as he does not stop to examine minutely, than one who has never been taught to look upon what he sees with an intention of reproducing a likeness of it. The attention to the exact shape of the whole, and the proportion of the parts, which is requisite for the taking of an adequate sketch, is converted into a habit, and becomes productive both of instruction and amusement.'*

Again, in reference to the lessons on number, which, as represented by Ramsauer, must have been most monotonous and without interest, it is necessary to bear in mind that Pestalozzi's theory is quite different from his practice. He based his arithmetical methods on the principle that the child should acquire his knowledge from the actual counting of things, and find out the various rules experimentally. If the spirit of this method is realized by the teacher, nothing can be more important than the influence it has upon his instruction in the subject. Treated in a practical and common sense manner, arithmetic is invaluable as a mental discipline, and instead of being a dry task, it is rendered an interesting exercise. Base all your lessons in arithmetic, then, upon things, concrete objects, peas, pens, pencils. The numerical tables, mentioned by Ramsauer, were superseded by the ball-frame, now in common use. The earliest introduction of the Pestalozzian arithmetic into Britain was into

* " Letters on Early Education," xxiv, p. 117.

the Dublin model schools, by the Irish Commissioners, who published an edition of the manual of exercises for the use of their teachers. A somewhat modified form of their manual was published in 1844, under the sanction of the Committee of Council on Education. That work was superseded by Tate's "First Principles of Arithmetic," a work which gave a more correct and comprehensive application of Pestalozzi's principles to the study of arithmetic, and which has done much to improve the system of teaching the subject in elementary schools.

Ramsauer adds to the interest of his narrative by giving a pen and ink sketch of Pestalozzi's personal appearance, which, as we learn from other sources, was not prepossessing. Imagine a little man with rugged face, his head well sunk in between his shoulders, but his eye bright and beaming, whose entire neglect of his person and his dress, and all matters of etiquette, as his own love letter confesses, increased his natural disadvantages, and you have a fair picture of Pestalozzi. In reading the account of Ramsauer and others, we take up the impression of a man who was never to be seen without a flushed face and excited look, who could do nothing calmly and quietly. 'The first time that I was taken into Pestalozzi's school,' he relates (being at that time ten years of age), 'he cordially welcomed and kissed me with his strong prickly beard, and having assigned me a place, he kept on reading out sentences without halting for a moment. As I did not understand a bit of what was going on, when I heard the word "monkey, monkey," come every time at the end of a sentence, and as Pestalozzi, who was very ugly, ran about the room as if he was wild, without a coat and without a neckcloth, his long shirt sleeves hanging down over his arms and hands, which swung negligently about, I was seized with real terror, and might soon have believed that he himself was a monkey.' (Raumer, p. 38.)

In spite of his ungainly appearance, however, the personal influence of the man was very great; as there was a spirit and a power in his very look which was quite irresistible. To this fact Ramsauer strongly testifies—

'In Burgdorf, an active and entirely new mode of life opened to me; there reigned so much love and simplicity in the institution; the life was so genial—I could almost say patriarchal; not much was learned, it is true, but Pestalozzi was the father, and the teachers were the friends of the pupils; his morning and evening prayers had such a fervour and simplicity, that they carried away every one who took part in them;

he prayed fervently, read and explained Gellert's hymns impressively, exhorted each of the pupils individually to private prayer, and saw that some pupils said aloud in the bedrooms every evening the prayers which they had learned at home, while he explained at the same time that the mere repeating of prayers by rote was worthless, and that every one should rather pray from his own heart.'

A pulmonary attack obliged Pestalozzi to give up his appointment in the elementary school, and after his recovery he founded an educational institution in the Castle of Burgdorf, which was opened in 1800. While there he wrote one of his most celebrated works, "How Gertrude Teaches her Children," from which I have already made several quotations. The most remarkable principles laid down in this book are the following :—
(1) The foundation of teaching is *shewing* (demonstration). (2) In every branch, teaching should begin with the simplest elements, and should proceed from these by steps suited to the child's development, observing in regard to this the laws of psychology. (3) The teacher should dwell on each point till the matter of instruction becomes the free mental possession of the pupil. (4) The acquisition of knowledge and skill is not the chief end of elementary

teaching, but the development and strengthening of the mental powers. (5) The relation between pupil and teacher, especially also the school discipline, should be based on and be regulated by *love*. (6) Teaching should keep in view the purpose of education.*

Excellent as these principles are, we are painfully aware that in many instances Pestalozzi failed to carry them into practice. What could be worse, for example, than the following? 'Lessons in names,' he says, 'consist in giving the children lists of the names of the most important objects in all three kingdoms of nature, in history and geography, and in the pursuits and relations of mankind. These lists of words are placed in the hands of the child merely as exercises in learning to read, immediately after he has gone through his spelling-book; and experience has shewn me that it is possible to make the children so thoroughly acquainted with these lists of words that they shall be able to repeat them from memory, merely in the time that is required to perfect them in reading.'

It is not even hinted here that the children ought to know the *things* named; *words*, mere *words*, are put in the place of observation. His directions, again, for teaching geography would

* Morf, pp. 258-270.

resolve themselves, in the case of England, into something like the following—

'The child should first be made familiar with its division into forty counties, with a number attached to each county. After this the child is to be supplied with an alphabetical list of the towns in England, every town on the list having beside it the number of the county to which it belongs, *e.g.*, Abergavenny, 16; Alnwick, 29, and on these he is to be constantly exercised until he is able to determine the place of all the towns in England.' What could be more artificial and unrealistic than this? and, besides, there is not a word said about *maps*. This reference may fitly close my notice of this famous book, which contains educational views of the highest value and importance, side by side with the most glaring blunders and absurdities.

The institution at Burgdorf was visited by numbers of people, who came even from a distance, attracted by the perusal of this interesting book. In 1802, the institution was recognized by Government, and obtained a grant of money, and Pestalozzi, now in the height of his fame, was elected as a deputy to represent Switzerland at Paris. While in the French capital it is related that, with his usual enthusiasm, he put a memorandum on the wants of Switzerland into the hands of

Napoleon, then First Consul, but he paid as little attention to it as he did to Pestalozzi's educational efforts, declaring that he could not mix himself up with the teaching of the A B C. His stay was very brief. 'I have been in Paris, too,' he used to say, 'but at night, and I did not see it.'

In consequence of political changes, Pestalozzi was obliged to clear out of the Castle of Burgdorf in 1804, and was offered instead the Monastery of Buchsee, which was put into proper order for the reception of his institution. Close by Buchsee lay the estate of Hofwyl, where De Fellenberg resided; and to him the teachers gave the chief direction of affairs, 'not without my consent,' says Pestalozzi, 'but to my profound mortification.' As these two men may justly be regarded as the originators of the modern educational movement in Europe, it may not be out of place here to give a few points of resemblance and of difference in their talents and characters. Their efforts, as we know, took the same direction, the amelioration of society, to which they both devoted their lives. Experience had brought both to the conclusion that this amelioration was to be hoped for only from an improved and extended education for all classes, particularly for the poor; and with this object in view, they each founded and personally conducted educational institutions, which they intended to serve as models for general imitation. They agreed in many of their opinions on educational method, Fellenberg having adopted several principles directly from Pestalozzi, who was his senior by a quarter of a century. They resembled each other also in possessing, in a high degree, the qualities of enthusiasm, energy, perseverance, and moral courage. They had each to encounter much opposition, and to overcome many difficulties; but nothing could turn them from their purpose, or abate their ardour. Here the parallel ends, and the points of difference begin. Pestalozzi was the greater man in that he had genius, sensibility, and imagination, in addition to the qualities which were common to both. His literary works prove that he combined many of the highest qualities of the philosopher and the poet. Fellenberg, on the other hand, had no literary powers, but he possessed a class of qualities in which Pestalozzi was singularly deficient, and which are indispensable to the success of practical undertakings on a large scale. He had a thoroughly disciplined mind, great firmness of will, a sound judgment, remarkable sagacity, keen powers of calculation, foresight, inventive skill, governing tact—in short, all the qualifications which constitute a successful administrator. Thus it happened that while Pestalozzi's undertakings frequently failed, Fellenberg's generally succeeded. Pestalozzi brought ruin and misery upon himself and his family; Fellenberg enriched himself. The life of Pestalozzi was sorely troubled by unseemly contentions among his assistants; around Fellenberg everything worked harmoniously. Pestalozzi often contradicted his theory in attempting to apply it to practice; with Fellenberg theory and practice always went hand in hand. Pestalozzi allowed his enthusiasm and his genial temper to lead him into all sorts of extravagancies; Fellenberg, though a man of strong passions, rarely acted impulsively. This remarkable dissimilarity between the two men was no doubt owing, in a great measure, to a difference in their natural endowment, but it was also the result of a difference of education. Fellenberg had enjoyed the counsel, control, and example of a well educated father, who carefully trained him for the duties of active life. Pestalozzi was early deprived of the blessings of a father's influence, which no other person can well supply. In the stirring politics of the times in which they lived, the two men took opposite sides—Pestalozzi, sprung from the middle classes, and indignant at the harsh and oppressive rule of the aristocracy, was an adherent of the reforming party, and welcomed the French Revolution; Fellenberg, by birth a member of the aristocracy, was one of the most active in resisting the French invasion, and had to flee for his life. He did not approve, however, of the exclusive pretensions of his order, whom he advised to win back the alienated affections of the peasantry by showing a noble zeal for the safety of their country. The main difference between the educational views of the two men was this, Pestalozzi taught that the object of national education should be to develop the mental and moral faculties of every individual member of society, without distinction of rank. This cultivation of the general intelligence of the children of the nation, he maintained, should be the foundation for the special education needed to qualify them for any particular rank or pursuit. Fellenberg adopted this principle in the main, but held that Pestalozzi carried it too far. He maintained that the general culture should apply only to the earliest period of a child's education, which should be limited in its duration by the capacity and circumstances in life of each individual; and that this preliminary training should be followed by one chiefly devoted to the acquisition of such positive knowledge as would fit him for the discharge of his duties as a member of society. This principle of adapting the education of the pupil to the requirements of his probable station and occupation in after-life commends itself at once to practical minds as a sound and important one ; nor is it at all at variance with the Pestalozzian principle of general development, for the teaching of almost any branch of knowledge may be so conducted as to have a highly educative influence on the mind of the learner. This modification has accordingly been adopted by the great majority of Pestalozzi's followers in Germany and elsewhere.*

It is not a matter of wonder, therefore, that Pestalozzi accepted in 1805 a highly advantageous proposal from the inhabitants of Yverdun, that he should open an educational institution in their town, and here it was that his fame reached its highest point. Visitors were attracted from all parts of Europe, and schools, on the model of Pestalozzi's, were started in Madrid, Naples, and St. Petersburg. The Emperor of Russia gave him a personal proof of his favour and esteem, and Fichte declared, in his "Addresses to the German Nation," that he saw in Pestalozzi and his labours the dawning of a new era for humanity. In 1808, the most hopeless period of the history of Germany, Fichte addressed a Prussian audience in Berlin, and

* I am indebted for this parallel to an article by Mr. Tilleard in the "Museum" for 1861.

called upon them, and upon all his countrymen, to look the humiliation of their country fairly in the face, and devise remedies for her salvation. 'Political resistance,' he cried, 'was now in vain, and the only hope that remained for them to cherish was their hope in the rising generation. They must live, not for themselves, but for the upbringing and education of this generation. It is education alone, the education of a worthy posterity, that can save us from the evils by which we are oppressed.'

In reading this stirring address in the light of the eventful history of 1870 and 1871, one feels how far-seeing Fichte was, and his heart beats high at the glorious success which crowned sixty years of a nation's educational efforts. Happy is the nation that possesses a Fichte in its hour of despair, and happier still if it can lay the lesson of its despair to heart, and take the advice so nobly proffered.

Fichte's words made a deep impression on a young man named Carl Von Raumer, then resident at Paris, and absorbed at the same moment in reading "How Gertrude Teaches her Children." Moved by Fichte's words, and by Pestalozzi's book, Raumer made up his mind to visit Yverdun in person, and get himself trained for the work which every patriotic German was now called upon to undertake. And Raumer was specially qualified for the task. He had already studied at Göttingen and Halle, and had devoted several years to the practical study of mineralogy. His account of what he saw in Pestalozzi's school, accordingly, is that of an intelligent and experienced eye-witness, and his estimate of Pestalozzi's genius and character is acknowledged to be both faithful and unbiassed. It is contained in a large work of his, entitled, "Geschichte der Pädagogik," a history of educational science, which is generally considered to be the best of its kind. The article on Pestalozzi was translated some years ago by Mr. Tilleard of the Council Office, and to this I have been greatly indebted in writing this chapter.

It was towards the close of October, 1809, that Raumer reached the institution at Yverdun, the situation of which was beautiful in the extreme. An extensive meadow separated it from the southern end of the glorious Lake of Neufchatel, on the west side of which rose the Jura Mountains, covered with vineyards. He was conducted to Pestalozzi; and he describes him as being 'dressed in the most negligent manner, having on an old grey overcoat, but no waistcoat, and his stockings were hanging down over his slippers; his coarse, bushy, black hair uncombed and frightful; his brow deeply furrowed, his dark brown eyes now soft and mild, and now full of fire. You hardly noticed that the old man, so full of geniality, was ugly; you read in his singular features long continued suffering and great hopes.'

Equally graphic descriptions are given of Pestalozzi's assistants; Niederer, who gave Raumer the impression of a young Roman Catholic priest; Krüsi, who was somewhat corpulent, fair, blue eyed, mild, and benevolent; and Schmid, who was, if possible, more cynical in his dress than Pestalozzi, with sharp features, and eyes like those of a bird of prey; all notable men in the personal history of Pestalozzi. There were at this time in the institution 165 pupils, of ages varying from six to seventeen, about half of whom were Swiss, the rest German, French, Prussian, Italian, Spanish, and American. In addition there were fifteen teachers, and thirty-two persons who may be designated students in training to be teachers. None of the teachers had a sitting room to himself, and Raumer states that when he had any private work to do, he had to do it while standing at a writing desk in the midst of the tumult of a class. His expectations, which had perhaps been too high, were not realized. Among other things, he expected to find a spirit of cordial love and concord reigning throughout, and that the place would be, as it were, a school for cultivating domestic affection and unity. Such, alas! was the ideal in Pestalozzi's mind, but the actual facts fell far short of it. Indeed, the tone of the school was one more of pushing and driving than of domestic peace. And the source of this discrepancy is not far to seek: it lay manifestly in the fact that while Pestalozzi's ideal comprehended the amelioration of the whole human race, he had not the requisite ability for conducting even the smallest village school. Nay, his highly active imagination led him to consider and describe, as actually existing in the institution, whatever he hoped sooner or later to see realized. His hopeful spirit foresaw future development in what was already accomplished, and he expected that others would benevolently see the same. This bold assumption had an effect on many, especially on the teachers of the institution; and this fact explains how in Pestalozzi's reports on the institution and on his system, so much could be said *bonâ fide*, which a sober spectator was forced to pronounce untrue. The concern which Pestalozzi felt in regard to the reputation of his establishment became painfully apparent when foreigners, particularly persons of distinction, visited Yverdun. Ramsauer, who was a teacher here as well as at Burgdorf, gives the following graphic account of the results of the old man's feeling in this respect :—

'As many hundred times in the course of the year, as foreigners visited the Pestalozzian Institution, so many hundred times did Pestalozzi allow himself, in his enthusiasm, to be deceived by them. On the arrival of every fresh visitor, he would go to the teachers in whom he placed most confidence and say to them, "This is an important personage, who wants to become acquainted with all we are doing. Take your best pupils and their analysis books (copy-books in which the lessons were written out), and show him what we can do, and what we wish to do." Hundreds and hundreds of times there came to the institution silly, curious, and often totally uneducated persons, who came because it was the "fashion." On their account, we usually had to interrupt the class instruction, and hold a kind of examination. In 1814, the aged Prince Esterhazy came. Pestalozzi ran all over the house, calling out, " Ramsauer, Ramsauer, where are you ? Come directly with your best pupils to the Red House (the hotel at which the Prince had alighted). He is a person of the highest importance, and of infinite wealth ; he has thousands of bond slaves in Hungary and Austria. He is certain to build schools, and set free his slaves, if he is made to take an interest in the matter." I took about fifteen pupils to the hotel. Pestalozzi presented me to the Prince with these words: "This is the teacher of these scholars, a young man who, fifteen years ago, migrated with other poor children from the canton of Appenzell, and came to me. But he received an elementary education, according to his individual aptitudes, without let or hindrance. Now he is himself a teacher. Thus you see that there is as much ability in the poor as in the richest, frequently more; but in the former it is seldom developed, and even then, not methodically. It is for this reason that the improvement of the popular schools is so highly important. But he will shew you everything we do better than I could. I will, therefore, leave him with you for the present." I now examined the pupils, taught, explained, and bawled in my zeal till I was quite hoarse, believing that the Prince was thoroughly convinced about everything. At the end of an hour, Pestalozzi returned. The Prince expressed his pleasure at what he had seen. He then took leave; and Pestalozzi, standing on the steps of the hotel, said, " He is quite convinced, quite convinced, and will certainly establish schools on his Hungarian estates." When we had descended the stairs, Pestalozzi said, "Whatever ails my arm? It is so painful. Why, see! it is quite swollen, I can't bend it!" And in truth his wide sleeve was now too small for his arm. I looked at the key of the house door of the *Maison Rouge*, and said to Pestalozzi, " Look here, you struck yourself against this key when we were going to the Prince an hour ago." On closer observation, it appeared that Pestalozzi had actually bent the key by hitting his elbow against it. In the first hour afterwards he had not noticed the pain, for the excess of his zeal and joy. So ardent and zealous was the good old man, already numbering seventy years, when he thought he had an opportunity of doing good! I could adduce many such instances. It was nothing rare in summer for strangers to come to the Castle four or five times in the same day, and for us to have to interrupt the instruction two, three, or four times.'

The contradiction previously referred to, and, in addition, the personal quarrels of the teachers, gradually sealed the fate of the institution. A spirit of opposition soon sprang up against it. The public journals, as Pestalozzi himself acknowledges, reported that 'what we did was by no means what we considered and represented ourselves to be doing ; but, instead of penitently retiring to modesty, we sturdily resisted this opposition.' Persisting in this folly, Pestalozzi and his staff pressed for a formal examination by the State; and a commission of inquiry went, and remained five days—'five sultry days' for Pestalozzi and his teachers. The report subsequently issued, though without doubt impartial, was not quite favourable; and after its publication there arose a long and violent literary warfare, which did anything but add to the credit of the institution. Fortunately we have the valuable testimony of Raumer, which may be accepted as in the main trustworthy. He attributes the failure of the institution to two or three causes, the chief of which was—(1) the one already indicated, that the family or domestic character was not sufficiently preserved, of which Raumer had painful proof from observing that Freddy, a little boy whom he had taken with him, led a cold and uncomfortable existence, which grieved and troubled him much. (2) Many of the teachers were unskilled and insufficiently educated, and in many cases ambitious to 'try their prentice hand' at new methods and new plans, and their chief did not try to remedy the evil by giving them lectures and training them in the practice of school teaching, both of which courses are imperatively necessary, and are now carried out in every training school. (3) Pestalozzi's views of what a teacher should be were not high—in fact, he laboured under the mistaken notion that a teacher had nothing to do but 'take his scholars through a compendium, following the directions how to use it, without adding thereto, or diminishing therefrom. He was never required to be more than just a step in advance of the scholars. Just as if a guide with a lantern were to be given to a man travelling in the night, and the guide had not only to light the traveller, but first to find out the way himself with the aid of the lantern.'

No wonder that Raumer, who went about listening and observing attentively in silence, declares that in moments of sadness the institution appeared to him like a great noisy education factory. On one occasion, Pestalozzi came to him and said, ' My teachers are afraid of you, because you only listen and look on in silence ; why do you not teach ?' ' I answered that before teaching I wished to learn—to learn in silence. Pestalozzi pressed me to teach mineralogy, and in doing so to make use of a small collection of minerals which the institution possessed. I replied that, if I did so, I must entirely depart from the methods of instruction pursued in the institution. How so ? asked Pestalozzi. According to that method, I replied, I should have nothing to do but to hold up before the boys one specimen of the collection after another, to give the name of each, for example, "that is chalk," and thereupon to make the class repeat in unison three times, "that is chalk." It was thought that in this way the observation of actual objects and instruction in language were provided for at the same time.

'I endeavoured to explain that such a mode of instruction made a mere show, giving children words before they had formed an idea of the images of the minerals; that moreover this process of perception and conception was only disturbed by the talking of the teacher and the repetition of the scholars, and was therefore best done in silence. On Pestalozzi's opposing this view, I asked him why children are born speechless, and do not begin to learn to speak until they are about three years old; why we should in vain hold a light before a child eight days old, and say "light" three times, or even a hundred times, as the child would certainly not try to repeat the word; whether this was not an indication to us from a higher hand, that time is necessary for the external perception of the senses to become internally appropriated, so that the word shall only come forth as the matured fruit of the inward conception now fully formed. What I said about the silence of children struck Pestalozzi.'

Raumer left the school in May, 1810; soon after the other teachers retired one by one; the brilliancy of its reputation decreased more and more, and in 1817 its affairs came to a crisis. How clear and cutting is the reproach of Niederer, in a letter written to Pestalozzi in March, 1818: 'Ruin entered your institution,' he exclaims, 'when, dazzled and led away by individual instances of brilliant talents and results, you ceased to bestow any particular attention on that which by its nature can work only in silence, though it stands higher than talent, and alone can render the development of talent possible ; when you began to act as if you owed everything to that with which you could make a display, and nothing to that which was not suited to this purpose.'

This lays down clearly, as on a chart, the rock on which Pestalozzi split, and which brought the institution at Yverdun to an unhonoured close. Thus terminated the last of Pestalozzi's important educational undertakings ; his wife, faithful and patient to the end, had died in 1811, and was buried under two walnut trees in the garden of the Castle ; and, in 1825, Pestalozzi himself, an old man of eighty years, and weary of life, retired to Neuhof, where exactly half a century before he had begun his first poor school. Before he died he wrote the " Fortunes of My Life," looking back with much pain on his many shipwrecked enterprises, and acknowledging that the blame had been his own, that the wreck of his life had been brought on by his incompetency to manage the helm. On the 17th February, 1827, he came to his grave in a full age, like as a shock of corn cometh in his season (Job v, 26), and over the grave where he rests from his toilsome labours, the following epitaph has been inscribed by his admiring countrymen :—

> 'TO OUR FATHER PESTALOZZI.
>
> Here reposes Henry Pestalozzi.
> Born at Zurich, 12th January, 1746.
> Died at Brugg, 17th February, 1827.
> Saviour of the poor at Neuhof.
> Father of the orphans at Stanz.
> Founder of new schools for the people at Burgdorf.
> Teacher of humanity at Yverdun.
> A man, a Christian, a citizen.
> Everything for others, for himself nothing.
> Peace to his ashes !'

At Pestalozzi's grave we forget his faults ; and in spite of his faults we love the man. His personal influence on methods of teaching was small, but his principles have taken deep root. He compelled the scholastic world to revise the whole of its task, or, to use his own forcible expression, 'he turned the European education vessel round, and put it in a new track.' His spirit has been infused into whole generations of teachers in his native land, and into numberless disciples far and wide over the civilized world. The great development of education in England during the past half century is in a great measure due to his influence. The earliest minutes of the Education Department recognise the merit of his principles, and offer practical suggestions to teachers directly based upon them.* It was on the model of the institutions founded by Pestalozzi and Fellenberg that Sir James Kay Shuttleworth and Mr. Tufnell founded the Battersea Normal School, one of the earliest of its kind in this country. The Home and Colonial School Society, also, by whom so much has been done for the improvement of infant education, have professedly been guided by his example.†

Perhaps the gravest mistake Pestalozzi made in his whole system of teaching was his failing to base his instruction on the life-giving principles of Christianity. A Christian he was no doubt, but religious teaching held too little place in his system. It was the moral sense which Pestalozzi sought to honour and to develop—and having faith, like Rousseau and Bäsedow, in the innate nobility of human nature and in its perfectibility through good influences and training, he

* " Minutes," 1840, 1841.
† See Bartley's " Schools for the People," pp. 8, 9.

takes no account of man's natural depravity, of the vicious elements which Christianity presupposes, which observation makes known to us, and on which education should act with a view to their reformation. Like Rousseau, Pestalozzi sought to gather figs of thorns, and, as a consequence, reaped only the bitterer fruit.*

The following is Pestalozzi's estimate of what a teacher should be :—'The schoolmaster should at least be an open-hearted, cheerful, affectionate, and kind man, who would be as a father to the children ; a man made on purpose to open children's hearts and their mouths, and to draw forth their understandings, as it were, from the hindermost corner. In most schools, however, it is just the contrary. The schoolmaster seems as if he were made on purpose to shut up children's mouths and hearts, and to bury their good understandings ever so deep under ground. That is the reason why healthy and cheerful children, whose hearts are full of joy and gladness, hardly ever like school.' (Biber, p. 147.) And his opinion of the duty of teachers to interest: 'An interest in study is the first thing which a teacher

---

* On the judgment of the Conservative School on the influence of Pestalozzi, see " De l'Education Populaire, par Eugène Rendu," pp. 191, 193.

should endeavour to excite and keep alive. There are scarcely any circumstances in which a want of application in children does not proceed from a want of interest; and there are perhaps none in which the want of interest does not originate in the mode of teaching adopted by the teacher. I would go so far as to lay it down as a rule, that wherever children are inattentive, and apparently take no interest in a lesson, the teacher should always first look to himself for the reason. There is a most remarkable reciprocal action between the interest which the teacher takes, and that which he communicates to his pupils. If he is not with his whole mind present at the subject, if he does not care whether he is understood or not, whether his manner is liked or not, he will alienate the affections of his pupils, and render them indifferent to what he says. But real interest taken in the task of instruction—kind words and kinder feelings—the very expression of the features, and the glance of the eye, are never lost upon children.' *

Whether we turn to French, German, or English estimates, the panegyrics on Pestalozzi's character are equally strong. In the words of Eugène Rendu, 'we cannot but render homage to the man whose life was a constant immolation

* " Letters on Early Education," xxx, p. 150.

of self.' Fichte says, 'Pestalozzi must needs remain in the history of our age one of the most extraordinary and beautiful phenomena. This his contemporaries feel; posterity will appreciate it still more deeply.' Mr. Tilleard, in an article in the "Encyclopedia Britannica," remarks, ' His enthusiastic love for children; his zealous devotion to the interests of his countrymen and of humanity; his unswerving faith in the efficacy of education (under God's blessing) for the regeneration of the lower classes of society; his unflinching courage in urging upon rulers, and all set in authority, the sacred duty of providing for the poor a more Christian institution than either the workhouse or the gaol; above all, the intense concentration of energy and purpose with which he pursued his object through a long and often unhappy life : those features in his character demand our highest admiration, and place Pestalozzi in the foremost rank of distinguished schoolmasters.' *

* The most recent biography of Pestalozzi is that by H. Morf, of Winterthur. This book affords the best picture that has been drawn of Pestalozzi, doing ample justice to his character and his labours. His complete works are to be had in a new, cheap, and correct edition by the Rev. L. W. Seyffarth, published at Brandenburgh.

DR. ANDREW BELL.

Sketch of his Life—School at Madras—Invention of the Monitorial System—Publication of "an Experiment on Education".—Details of the Monitorial System—Its Introduction—Modes of Discipline—Successful Teaching—The "Paidometer"—Monitorial System, pro and con—Its chief Advocates—Introduction into England—The "Bell and Lancaster" Controversy—Mrs. Trimmer—National Society—British and Foreign School Society—Chairs of Education.

IN the case of Dr. Bell, Scotland can boast of giving birth to an educationist, of whom Southey wrote a flattering biography, in three volumes, and whose fame obtained for him a resting-place in Westminster Abbey, where an elegant monument characterizes him as the 'Author of the Madras System.' When the teacher learns, further, that this educationist professes to show him a plan, whereby a school may teach itself under the superintendence of the master, he is naturally anxious to sit down and listen attentively to what he has to say. But whether the system justifies the professions of its author, the reader must judge for himself.

Born at St. Andrews, in 1753, Dr. Bell was educated at the university there, went to America, and, after a short residence there, returned to England, and took orders in the Episcopal Church. After acting as minister at Leith for a short time, a position which did not satisfy him, he set out for India in 1787, thinking that he might there turn his acquirements in natural philosophy to good account, in the way of lecturing and teaching. On his arrival at Madras he was favourably received, and met with considerable encouragement, as he says himself, 'in the line of the Church.' Among other offices to which he was appointed, most of them sinecures, but none of them, as a critic remarks, 'sine salaries,'* was that of chaplain to the garrison; and in this capacity it was that he had an opportunity of displaying his inventive genius in the work of education. A school for educating the orphan children of European soldiers had shortly before been established at Madras, and to Dr. Bell, as chaplain, the superintendence of this school was committed. A good salary was offered to him; but this, to his credit be it said, he firmly and persistently declined, as he considered the task of instructing

* " Dunn's Sketches," p. 27.

the young to be one of his chief duties as a clergyman. The difficulties he had to encounter were of the most unpromising kind ; the children, who were half-caste, were inferior both in moral and intellectual faculties, and the teachers were so wedded to their own mode of teaching, or, 'so much oppressed by the lethargy incident to a tropical climate,' that they declined to carry out the plans he proposed. As he pondered over the perplexities of his position, and looked in vain for a solution of his difficulties, he chanced, on one of his morning rides, to pass by a Malabar school, where he observed the children seated on the ground, and writing with their fingers in sand. He hastened home, repeating as he went 'I have it now,' and gave immediate orders to the ushers of the lowest classes to teach the alphabet in the same manner, sand being provided, and strewn upon a board. This order met with the usual reception, the ushers declaring the thing to be impossible. But the doctor was not to be daunted. Despairing of help from his teachers, he bethought himself of employing a boy, on whose obedience, disposition, and cleverness he could rely, and giving him charge of the alphabet class. The lad's name was John Frisken (the name of the first monitor in English education is deserving of honourable mention), the son of a soldier, and then about eight years old. Dr. Bell gave him the necessary directions, and told him that he looked to him for success. What the usher had declared to be impossible, the lad succeeded in effecting without any difficulty. The alphabet class made rapid progress, and Frisken was appointed its permanent teacher. Following out his experiment, Dr. Bell appointed other boys to be assistant teachers to the lower classes, giving to Frisken oversight of the whole, because of his intelligence and experience. Similar improvement was noticed in these classes, as had taken place in teaching the alphabet, a result which Dr. Bell attributed to the diligence and fidelity with which his little friends, as he used to call them, carried out his orders. To them a smile of approbation was no mean reward, and a look of displeasure sufficient punishment. In the joy of his heart, Dr. Bell proceeded to apply his system of monitors to the whole school; the master and ushers being gradually superseded. The precise date of this experiment, the germ of our present excellent system of pupil teachers, cannot be ascertained, but it may be taken with sufficient accuracy to have been not later than 1791.*

The results achieved by this system of teaching

* Southey's "Life of Dr. Bell," vol. I.

were most satisfactory. In 1794, Dr. Bell wrote to a friend in the following terms: "The school promises fair to present to me the sole reward I have sought of all my labours with my young pupils, by giving to society an annual crop of good and useful subjects, many of them rescued from the lowest state of depravity and wretchedness."* In point of learning, too, the boys soon advanced far beyond their original masters, and were instructed in arithmetic, vulgar and decimal fractions, book-keeping, grammar, geography, geometry, mensuration, navigation, and astronomy. One of them, William Smith, attended the embassy to Tippoo Saib, when his sons the hostage princes were restored, and went through a course of experiments in natural philosophy in presence of the Sultan, who detained the youth after the embassy had taken leave, that he might instruct two of his courtiers in the use of Dr. Bell's set of philosophical apparatus, which had been purchased and presented to him by the Government of Madras, an incident which was wrought into a story by Miss Edgeworth, author of "Practical Education," and appears in her popular tales under the title of "Lame Jervas." Mr. Edgeworth, her father, at that time a Commissioner on Irish education, having written to

* "Abridged Works of Dr. Bell," by Bishop Russell, p. 32.

him in 1806 for advice on various matters, Dr. Bell disclaims ability to recommend books on the subject of education, to a man who had read so much, and adds: 'There is only one book which I have studied, and which I take the liberty to recommend. It is a book in which I have learned all I have taught, and infinitely more; a book open to all alike, and level to every capacity, which only requires time, patience, and perseverance, with a dash of zeal and enthusiasm in the perusal—I mean *a school full of children.*'

The change produced on the character of his pupils had an immediate effect on their condition and their prospects in life; and they were eagerly sought for, to fill situations of considerable trust and emolument. The school became deservedly popular, and the Government, being sensible of the beneficial tendency of the system of teaching pursued in it, and of its ready adaptation to all schools of a similar kind, in which economy of time and of means was extremely important, took steps to extend it to other Presidencies. In the year 1796, the effect of climate began to tell on Dr. Bell's health and constitution to such a degree, that it became necessary for him to return to Europe. With this view he drew up a very full report on the state of the school, which was published in London in 1797, under the title of

"An Experiment in Education, made at the Male Asylum, Madras; suggesting a System by which a School or Family may Teach itself under the Superintendence of the Master or Parent," a report which gives minute directions as to the arrangements of the Madras school, and from which I now proceed to quote the most interesting and useful points.

I. In respect to organization, the school is divided into classes consisting of from twenty-five to thirty boys. Each class is paired off into tutors and pupils; thus, in a class of twelve boys, the six superior tutor the six inferior, each each, and in their seats the boys take their places in different order from that in which they stand in their class, as each pupil sits by the side of his tutor. 'Mark,' says the doctor, 'how many advantages grow out of this simple arrangement. From the moment you have nominated a boy a tutor, you have exalted him in his own eyes, and given him a character to support, the effect of which is well known. Next, the tutors enable their pupils to keep up with their classes, which, otherwise, some of them would fall behind, and be degraded to a lower class. Another advantage attending this arrangement is, that the tutor far more effectually learns his lesson than if he had not to teach it to another.'

There is undoubtedly a sound principle in this tutorial arrangement of Dr. Bell's, and every elementary teacher should take advantage of it, as far as is possible in the circumstances of his school; but the doctor omits to show how it is possible with the system of place-taking, which he adopted and strongly recommends, to secure a cordial "coaching" of the pupil by his tutor, when the very cordiality and success of the "coaching" might be the means of reversing the position of the tutor and pupil when lessons came to be said.

Again, each class has an assistant teacher (one of the senior boys), whose sole employment it is to instruct that class; to see that the tutors do their part; that they not only get their own lessons, but assist and forward their pupils, and, under the teacher, hear the whole class, tutors and pupils, say the lessons which they have assisted them in preparing. He sees at every instant how every boy in his class is employed, and hears every word uttered. This station of assistant was one of great emulation, being conferred only on such as performed their tasks with diligence, fidelity, and success.

The third grade in the rank of monitors was that of teacher, each of whom had charge of one or more classes. His business was to direct and guide the assistants, inspect their respective classes—the tutors and pupils—and see that all was maintained in good order, strict attention, and rigid discipline. The teacher must also hear each class say their lessons, or be present while the assistant does so. In cases where the assistant proves himself equal to the entire charge of his class, he is promoted to the rank of teacher. Of these teachers and assistants, there were fourteen in all at the Madras school for 200 boys, none of them less than seven, or more than fourteen years of age.

And what, under this system, were the duties of the schoolmaster? His province was to watch over and conduct the machine in all its parts and operations, and see the various offices just described carried into effect. From his place he overlooks the whole school, and gives life and motion to every member of it. He inspects the classes one by one, and is occupied wherever there is most occasion for his services, and where they will best tell. He is to encourage the diffident, the timid, and the backward, to check and repress the forward and presumptuous; to bestow just and ample commendation upon the diligent, attentive, and orderly, however dull their capacity, or slow their progress; to stimulate the ambitious, rouse the indolent, and make the idle bestir themselves; in short, to deal out praise and displeasure, encouragement and threatening, according to the temper, disposition, and genius of the scholar. He is occasionally to hear and instruct the classes, or rather overlook and direct the teachers and assistants while they do so. The advantage is, that not being perpetually occupied as in most schools in hearing and instructing one or other of the classes, which necessarily withdraws his attention for the time from the rest of the school, he has leisure to see that all are employed as they ought. The great advantage is that it is his chief business to see that others work, rather than work himself, and that he is most usefully employed in doing what men in general are most ready to do.*

These minute gradations of rank, devised for the purpose of making the school teach itself, are manifestly taken from the model of the army and navy, and Dr. Bell confesses this in his letter to Mr. Edgeworth, already referred to. 'Look at a regiment or a ship, and you will see a beautiful example of the system which I have recommended for a single school. Look at the army and navy, and you will see the grand system of superintendence which pervades all the

* "Abridged Works," *passim.*

works of men, and which will guide you in the general organization of your schools.'

Dr. Bell gives minute details of the methods which are to be observed in reducing his scheme to practice. Begin with arranging the school into classes. In large schools where great numbers have made equal progress, each class may consist of thirty-six scholars. In small schools there should be no more classes than the relative state of the scholars' progress absolutely requires. The fewer the classes the better.

The next step is to select the monitors of different grades from among the senior and best scholars. This is best done, if the master be not acquainted with the dispositions, characters, and attainments of the scholars, by the elective voice of the superior boys, and afterwards by means of the monitors selected, who scarcely ever fail to find for him the boy best fitted for his purpose. Their intimate knowledge of their school-fellows, and their being responsible to the master for their recommendation, are pledges of the faithful discharge of their task. The assistant teacher of a class may be the head boy of his own class, or a trusty boy of a superior class, and his appointment may be left to the option of his superior officer (the monitor teacher) when the latter has proved himself to be able and faithful. It is better to begin with a full share of teachers and assistants, and to diminish them, if necessary, when the school gets into order. The selection of the head monitors (styled teachers) brings the ability of the master to the test, for the discipline of the school, and the progress of the respective classes depend upon their capacity and diligence. And not only must the master be careful in selecting these, but he must exert his utmost vigilance and discretion in overlooking and directing all they do, and preventing or stopping on its first occurrence the smallest irregularity, deviation, or neglect. No teachers, who do not prove themselves equal to the task assigned to them, should be retained. The last step necessary is to pair each class into tutors and pupils— the head, or rather the best and most trusty boy, tutors the worst; the next best, the next worst, and so on. From time to time a new arrangement will be necessary when the pupils are found to gain upon their tutors; a point at which, as I have said, the Doctor's plan seems to be wanting in a knowledge of human nature. The pupil sits by the side of his tutor for instruction in his seat, but when the lessons are being heard by the teacher the boys range themselves in the order in which they left off at the end of the preceding lesson. (pp. 348-353.)

So much for the organization of a Madras school. The next subject of interest is its 'modes of discipline.' In the first place, the schoolmaster is furnished with a most powerful operator, the 'black book,' as the boys call it, or register of continued idleness, negligence, ill-behaviour, and every offence which requires serious investigation, and animadversion. To this instrument Bell attached immense importance in preserving order, diligence, good conduct, and the most rigid discipline at the least expense of punishment. The mode of working it seems to have been the following. When any serious offence occurred under the eye of any monitor, whether tutor, assistant, or teacher, it was his duty to report it to the schoolmaster, who was to use his discretion, whether to reprimand or threaten the culprit immediately, or to make a note in the register for future judgment. Omission to report an offence was considered a serious offence in itself; suppose a pupil committed an offence, deserving to be noted, and his tutor, though cognisant of it, failed to report it to the assistant or schoolmaster, the tutor was put down for neglect of duty. In like manner, if the tutor gave notice to the assistant, and the assistant did not to the teacher, the assistant was marked in the book; and so of the teacher. Also, if the assistant was guilty of misbehaviour, the teacher who witnessed it, and did not report it, was made responsible, and so on. On the other hand, any of the lower orders might report their superiors, as was often the case ; but no one in the link was called upon to do more than to report what he saw, and knew to be done contrary to the rules of the school, in the department committed to his charge, and for which he stood responsible.

In the second place, this register was inspected once a week, in presence of the whole school, drawn up in a circle for that purpose, when the nature and consequence of every omission and commission was explained in the language of the school. Each case brought up by book was usually decided, as it were, *by jury*, the boys around judging whether the culprit was innocent or guilty. The moral precepts, given by the schoolmaster on these occasions, being based on the actual offences recorded, produced a better effect in reaching the mind, and touching the heart, than abstract lectures could have done ; and the effect of the whole was much enhanced by the presence of the superintendent and visitors, who examined the school on these weekly occasions, and distributed rewards. This practice, no doubt, suggested to Stow his system of moral training lessons in gallery. The Doctor's system seems to reach the height of impracticability or absurdity in the following rule: 'When a bad lying boy comes to school, the teacher of the lower classes must find a good boy to take care of him, teach him right principles, treat him kindly, reconcile him to the school, and render him happy, like the rest, in his situation, and in his school, and playfellows.' (p. 117.) Out of doors, as well as in school, similar means were taken to secure good behaviour and discipline, and to teach the boys useful habits. For example, Dr. Bell took advantage of the ablutions necessary in a warm climate to teach them to swim; and if a boy, through fear, did not make progress in the art, he had a day set for him, on which he must shew a certain proficiency or be thrown into the tank out of his depth. The greater terror generally overcame the less; but, if not, care was taken to have the best swimmers collected round him to prevent any serious accident. A second ducking was never necessary to the same boy. The following incident, related in the Doctor's own words, affords sufficient proof that the moral influence of his disciplinary system was good.

'A boy of eight or nine years of age, stupid, sluggish, and pusillanimous, had been admitted into the school. The other boys made a mocking stock of him, and treated him with every insult and indignity. Inured to this treatment at his former school, he had no spirit to resist or even complain. As soon as I observed what was going on, and looked into the boy, it appeared to me that he would soon be confirmed in perfect idiotism, of which he had already the appearance. I summoned the boys as usual, and in their presence adopted the stranger as my *protégé*, because he stood most in need of protection. I told them that his disorder seemed to me to be in part owing to the manner in which he had been treated; and I spoke of the event which I apprehended from the continuance of such treatment. I pointed out the very different line of conduct which it was our duty to observe towards a fellow-creature and a fellow-Christian, and expressed a hope of the boy's improvement, if they would all treat him with marked kindness and encouragement. I enjoined them to change their demeanour towards him; and put him under the charge of a trusty boy, who was to explain to his pupil all that I had said. The result was wonderful. I had the satisfaction of seeing in good time the boy's countenance more erect and bright; his spirit, which had been completely broken, revived, and his mind, which had sunk into lethargy and stupidity, reanimated. Henceforth, his progress, though slow, was uniform and sure; and there was a good prospect of his becoming an inoffensive and useful member of society. (p. 123.)

Before leaving this subject, I must not omit to mention that Dr. Bell was strong against corporal punishment, and quotes Seneca, Quintilian, Plutarch, Locke, and Tillotson, as advocates against it.

Such were Dr. Bell's organization and discipline, which formed the best features of his system. In connection with the art of teaching, there is not much to record. The class work recommended by him is similar to what may be seen in every school at the present day. The principles on which he went were short, easy, frequent, or rather continued lessons, and that a boy never knows anything which is told him, or is improved by anything that is done for him; it is what he tells, and what he does for himself, which is alone useful. This enunciation of what I take to be the golden rule in all teaching, viz., that in all school work children should do as much as possible for themselves—in other words, *be trained*,—shews that Dr. Bell knew the secret of successful teaching. In giving lessons to beginners in the alphabet, and in the rudiments of writing, sand spread over a board was the medium used. 'The advantages of this plan,' he says, ' are many. It engages and amuses the mind, and so commands the attention, that it greatly facilitates the toil both of master and scholars." (p. 93.) In due time the child was promoted to paper, which he was on every occasion made to rule for his own use. Nor was any tutor or teacher allowed to write a single letter in the scholar's copy; everything had to be done by himself, even to the making and mending of the pen. He also adopted the excellent system of making the children syllabify the words—break them into syllables when reading—than which I know no better method for training children to acquire new or difficult words without help from the teacher. Another feature worthy of notice was the *marked book*. When a class was promoted to a new book, the master marked with pen and ink on the first page of those given to the monitors the number of the class, the monitor's name, the day of the month, and the manner in which it was to be read; and, in beginning each lesson for the day, the monitor was required to mark the day of the month, and also to make a note of the place where each successive lesson during the day began or ended. Then, at the close of the day, the master or teacher entered in a register the sum of the daily performances thus made, and these were added up weekly and monthly, and compared by the master or teacher with what was done the preceding day, week, and month. In the same register, called a paidometer, entries were made to note the proficiency of every individual. A similar plan was pursued with the copy and ciphering books.

Such are the main features of the Madras system, which attracted much attention in the early part of the present century, and of the importance of which greatly exaggerated estimates were formed and made public. Dr. Bell's own estimate is absurdly high. 'The system,' he says, 'has no parallel in scholastic history. In a school it gives to the master the hundred eyes of Argus, the hundred hands of Briareus, and the wings of Mercury. By multiplying his ministers at pleasure, it gives him indefinite powers; in other words, it enables him to instruct as many pupils as his school-room will contain.' (p. 171.) The very extravagance of the pretensions made by Bell, and his equally enthusiastic contemporary, Joseph Lancaster, led to a natural reaction, and for many years, and even now, teaching by monitors is decidedly unpopular among educationists. 'This system,' says Dr. Donaldson, rector of the High School of Edinburgh, 'ignores altogether the fact that the work of the teacher is to evolve the powers of the mind, and that for this work a wise and cultivated mind is required. In Prussia, there are neither monitors nor pupil teachers, a harmonious evolution of a human being being considered in that country a very important and difficult task; but in Lancaster's eyes this could be done quite well by a boy.'* But, I believe, with Mr. Fitch, H.M. Inspector of Schools, that both extremes of opinion are mistaken. 'Monitorial agency is not adapted, and never can be adapted for mental training of a very high order; but it is well calculated to facilitate much of the routine work of a large school, and by it, when well managed, a great deal of that work which is often regarded as drudgery by an adult, may be performed not only more economically but more cheerfully and not less efficiently than by any other method.' † A monitor, too, has naturally more sympathy with children, and is better able to explain many difficulties than an adult teacher; he can keep the younger children at work, and in good order, while the master directs his energies to the other work of the school; he is more patient in imparting knowledge, and more fertile in expedients for explaining and illustrating it; and, as I have remarked before, every teacher

* " Lectures on Education," p. 60.
† " Museum " for 1863.

should take advantage of it to the extent which the circumstances of his school will permit. In a family, also, much benefit may be derived from its adoption; if the parents superintend the home lessons, and train the elder children to teach the younger, they may ensure a considerable progress on the part of all, with little labour to themselves. Nor must it be forgotten that the monitor receives almost an equal benefit with the pupil—in fact, no one can be said to possess any knowledge thoroughly until he has imparted it to others.

Opinions favourable to the monitorial system have been expressed by various educationists. Professor Pillans bears the following testimony: 'Monitors are aware of the difficulties which they themselves encountered but lately, and are often able to explain them to their comrades in a manner more familiar and intelligible than can be done by the master, whose habits and ways of thinking are so widely different.' Father Girard, the benevolent founder of mutual instruction in Switzerland, says, that 'when he met with difficulty in explaining any word or subject to a child, he often called in a boy more advanced to aid him, and usually found him to succeed entirely, even when all his own efforts had failed.' Mr. Dunn, for many years Secretary to the British and Foreign School Society, observes that ' a monitorial school requires a better and abler teacher than almost any other; it demands more energy, more skill, more wisdom, and more strength, both of body and mind, and hence it not unfrequently happens that, when schools fail to accomplish the expectations of their founders, reproaches are cast upon the plan, which really belong to the agent, who has been vainly attempting to carry out arrangements, to the management of which he was altogether incompetent.'* Mr. Wyse, in his valuable work on " Education," passes an equally strong eulogy on the system.

On Dr. Bell's return to England, he was appointed Rector of the parish of Swanage, in Dorset, where he set himself to found Sunday schools, on the principles of his favourite system. He there met with difficulties similar to those experienced at Madras, and displayed the same zeal and perseverance, 'hammering directions into his scholars,' as an eye-witness expressed it, 'like a blacksmith on an anvil.' The system was tried in London, at Kendal, and elsewhere, but made little progress, till the doings of Joseph Lancaster, in a measure, 'dragged it into prominence.'† Lancaster had, about the same time, invented a monitorial plan of much the same

* " Principles of Teaching," p. 48.
† Lancaster's own words.

kind, and the claims of the rival systems excited quite a storm of controversy; and, strange to say, as in the case of the Trojan war, a woman was the originator of all the mischief. Mrs. Trimmer, a minor educationist of the period, was the first to suggest the idea that Lancaster's plans were inimical to the Church of England. 'From the time, sir,' she wrote to Dr. Bell, 'that I read Mr. Lancaster's "Improvements on Education," I conceived an idea that there was something in his plan inimical to the interests of the Established Church.' And then she adds, with charming innocence, 'and when I read your "Experiment on Education," I plainly perceived he had been building on your foundation.'* This roused the spirit of jealousy in Dr. Bell's breast, and put an end to the hitherto friendly relations between Lancaster and himself. Mrs. Trimmer was equally successful in alarming the church. 'This Lancaster,' she wrote, 'is a Goliath of schismatics, and if the church does not bestir itself, the education of the people will slip out of its hands into those of this Quaker.' And such a Quaker! 'It is a curious fact,' she adds, with delightful *naïveté*, 'that he was not originally a Quaker, but an Anabaptist. Whether he changed for the love of a pretty Quakeress, whom

* Southey's "Bell," vol. II.

he married, or whether the *broad brim* was the best cover for his scheme, I cannot say.' The alarm spread like wildfire over the length and breadth of the land; and church and chapel, bishop and dissenting minister, were ranged against each other, under the educational banner of Bell or Lancaster. Sermons were preached, voices were raised at public meetings, pamphlets were published (including several by the indefatigable Mrs. Trimmer), caricatures were exhibited of Bel and the Dragon, and the rival educators were upheld, by their respective partisans, as benefactors of their race, who had invented a panacea for the reformation of society and of the world. 'The country was divided into two great parties—the Lancasterians and the Bible, and the Bible only; and the followers of Bell, and the Church of England in danger. Southey and Coleridge, and the "Quarterly Review" denounced Lancaster and his system; but they had their match in Sydney Smith and Brougham, and the other writers of the "Edinburgh Review."' * It seems ludicrous that such a dust should have been raised over the fact that two enthusiastic gentlemen hit, about the same time, on a plan, that almost every teacher of a month's experience is sure to hit upon, for the instruction of his scholars.

* Donaldson's "Lectures," p. 63.

Did not Pestalozzi, about the same time, fall upon the method at Stanz? Had not the system been adopted in France, several years before, by the Chevalier Paulet, a gentleman, by the way, who adopted much the same modes of discipline as those recommended by Herbert Spencer.* And to go much farther back, it would appear from Plutarch that Lycurgus introduced a similar system of pedagogy in Sparta. It is sufficient, on the question of priority, to state that Lancaster himself acknowledges his indebtedness to Dr. Bell. In his first pamphlet, published in 1803, he writes: 'I ought not to close my account without acknowledging the obligations I lie under to Dr. Bell; I much regret that I was not acquainted with the beauty of his system, till somewhat advanced in my plan. If I had known it, it would have saved me much trouble and some retrograde movements.'

The sectarian storm that was raised bore the rival claimants on the crest of its waves; and fortunately it did not subside without giving a considerable impetus to the progress of education. In 1811 a society was formed for establishing schools in connection with the Church of England, and on Dr. Bell's system, called the National Society. Dr. Bell was appointed to act as superintendent in the formation of their

* "Edinburgh Review," vol. XXXIII, p. 489.

schools, and from this time till his death, his life blends with the progress of the society and its schools. To the duties of his office he devoted himself with unwearied zeal and assiduity, travelling extensively in the interests of the society, and labouring for the diffusion of his system with untiring energy. A similar society of Dissenters, called the British and Foreign School Society, was originated shortly afterwards, and each triumph of one or other spurred the flagging zeal of its rival. In this way the Madras system found a footing not only in England, but in Scotland and Ireland, and to a limited extent in America. To facilitate its introduction on the Continent, Dr. Bell made an extensive tour, in the course of which he visited the schools of Pestalozzi and Fellenberg. With Pestalozzi, he was quite charmed. 'He has much that is original,' he exclaims, ' much that is excellent. If he had a course of study—if he were to dismiss his masters and adopt the monitorial system, and the principle of emulation, he would be superexcellent.' *

This vanity, which formed a marked feature in his character, is perhaps pardonable in a man who sacrificed so much for the cause of education ; but one regrets to learn that his manner towards the teachers and managers of the schools

* Southey's " Bell," vol. III.

he visited was not courteous. Southey acknowledges that instead of delivering his instructions, and making his remarks in a gentlemanly and conciliatory way, his personal behaviour was such that he was almost universally dreaded and disliked. His treatment of the teachers in the presence of their pupils was frequently calculated to create any other sentiments than respect and attention. During his life, Dr. Bell received several lucrative offices in the Church, and having, perhaps, as strong a passion for money as for education, he amassed a sum of £120,000, which he bequeathed to various towns in his native country for the erection and maintenance of schools. To St. Andrews he bequeathed £60,000, the greater part of which was devoted to the foundation of the Madras College. An equal amount was divided betwixt Edinburgh, Glasgow, Aberdeen, Leith, and Cupar-Fife, in which Madras schools were established and are still maintained, though the monitorial system is no longer the chief feature in any of them. He also founded a lectureship at Edinburgh on the principles of teaching, and on the monitorial system, which was first filled by his biographer, Dr., afterwards Bishop Russell. This chair never attracted any notice, probably in consequence of its narrow basis in connection with the Theological Institution of the Episcopal Church; but following out the spirit of his will, and having received from Government a grant of money, by way of supplement to the funds at their own disposal, the Bell Trustees have recently founded chairs of education in the universities of Edinburgh and St. Andrews. Whether these chairs will exercise much influence on education remains to be seen, and will depend very much on the ability and judgment of the men who are selected to fill them; and on the scope which they propose for themselves in their lectures. If the professors occupy themselves with the higher principles of their subject, with the science and history of education, giving in their lectures the substance of all that has been written and said on education, and that has been carried into successful practice in the work of teaching; in short, if they be men who can introduce their students to the literature and the philosophy of the profession they have chosen, I anticipate good results from the establishment of these chairs.

Soon after making the princely donation referred to, Dr. Bell died at Cheltenham in 1832, and was buried in Westminster Abbey, the highest dignitaries of the Church and many eminent peers attending as mourners.

JOSEPH LANCASTER.

Antecedents—London Schools of the time—Opens a School in the Borough Road—Its Great Popularity—Monitorial System—Teaching to Read—Writing—Arithmetic—Modes of Discipline—Religious Teaching—Interview with the King—Prosperity and Extravagance—Lecturing Tours—Monitorial System tried in Agriculture—Resigns the Borough School—Difficulties and Death—Character and Work.

AFTER what has been said of the monitorial system in connection with Dr. Bell, little remains to be said of it coupled with Joseph Lancaster. Neither Bell's nor Lancaster's name is often heard in connection with education, yet both deserve a place in any gallery of educational portraits. Like Bell, Lancaster devoted his life to the spread of education, and it is hard to say which had most enthusiasm for the system which each claimed as his own. Bell used to say, 'Give me four-and-twenty children to-day, and I will supply you to-morrow with as many teachers.' 'By the aid of monitors,' exclaimed

Lancaster, 'one master can teach one thousand boys.' Both had greatly exaggerated notions as to the value of their discoveries, and wrought themselves into the belief that they were designed by Providence for the regeneration of mankind. But, in other respects, the characters of the men were widely different. Lancaster was imaginative and excitable, the creature of impulse, always, so to speak, 'on fire'; Bell was distinguished by decorum and worldly prudence. Lancaster was reckless and improvident in money matters; Bell was quite the opposite: the one died in debt and obscurity, the other wealthy and respected. But, 'of the rare diligence of Ascham, of the steadfast self-devotion and the clear insight into child-nature of Pestalozzi, of the high aims and manly earnestness of Arnold, we are not reminded as we read the life of either.'* 'Time has set its seal on the doings of both, and how different is the verdict to that which they so fondly anticipated! The *monitorial* principle survives, but their pretensions and eccentricities are forgotten.' †

Lancaster was born in Southwark in 1778. His father was a pensioner who had served in the American war, and, under his pious instruction, Lancaster was early imbued with a love for God,

* " Museum " for 1863. † Dunn's " Sketches."

and with a burning desire to devote himself to His service. It is possible, too, that his father's experience as a soldier may have suggested to Lancaster the almost military *régime* of his system of discipline. At the age of fourteen, Clarkson's "Essay on the Slave Trade" came in his way, and he was at once seized with a desire to set out for Jamaica and teach the poor blacks to read the Word of God. For this purpose he ran off from his parents, with a Bible and a "Pilgrim's Progress" in his pocket, but was in due time sent back by the captain of the ship on board which he had taken refuge. At the age of sixteen he looked forward to the Dissenting ministry, his religious views inclining him to the society of Quakers; but after teaching for a short time in private schools, he set himself with enthusiasm to the task of educating the poor, to which his attention was directed by the wretched state of the schools which then existed.

'There is a sort of initiatory or preparatory school,' he remarks, in his first tract on education, 'to be found in every part of London. They are frequented by boys and girls indiscriminately, few of them being above seven years of age. The mistress is frequently the wife of some mechanic, induced to undertake the task from a desire to increase a scanty income, or to add to her domestic comforts. The subjects of tuition are reading and needlework; the number of children is very fluctuating, and seldom exceeds thirty. The pay is very uncertain. Disorder and noise seem more the characteristics of these schools than improvement of any kind. Many poor children go at once from these schools to work, and have no other opportunities of instruction.'

Of the schools for older children, 'secondary schools,' as he calls them, his report is equally unfavourable.

'The masters of these are generally the refuse of superior schools, and too often of society at large. The pay and number of scholars are alike low and fluctuating: of course, there is little encouragement for steady men, either to engage or continue in this line, it being impossible to keep school, defray its expenses, and do the children regular justice without a regular income. Eventually many schools, respectable in better times, are abandoned to men of any character, who use as much chicane to fill their pockets as the most despicable pettifogger. Writing books are scribbled through, whole pages filled with scrawls, to hasten the demand for new books. These schools are chiefly attended by the children of artificers, whose pay fluctuates with their employ, and is sometimes withheld by bad principles. Debts are often contracted that do not exceed a few shillings; then the parents remove their children from school and never pay it, the smallness of the sum proving an effectual bar to its recovery; the trouble and loss of time being worse than the loss of money in the first instance.'

Moved by this pitiable state of matters, which the poet Crabbe describes very graphically in his " Schools of the Borough," Lancaster opened a school in 1798, at his father's house, which stood nearly opposite the present Borough Road Training College, into which this small beginning was destined eventually to grow. The course of instruction which he proposed to himself was reading, writing, arithmetic, and a knowledge of the Holy Scriptures, the fee being fourpence a week, about half that charged at most other schools. Yet, from the first, a good many were admitted free, for over his door was printed the announcement, 'All that will may send their children and have them educated freely; and those that do not wish to have education for nothing may pay for it, if they please.' He was then only twenty years of age, and knew no modes of teaching but those usually in practice; and for a time the school made only ordinary progress, the number in summer being about one hundred and twenty, and in winter fifty or sixty. In a season of scarcity many of the children were provided with dinner gratis, chiefly at the expense of a noble and generous-minded body of friends.* Such was Lancaster's first establishment, in which it is probable that, finding the old methods of teaching, to which he had been accustomed, totally inadequate, and puzzling himself what to do, he stumbled, as he himself expressed it, on a plan similar to Dr. Bell's, before he had seen the Madras Report. At all events, the little school which he had fitted up with his own hands, became too small for the numbers in attendance, and he had, in 1801, to remove to larger premises, which were provided for him on the site of the college already named, chiefly through the benevolent aid of the Duke of Bedford and Lord Somerville. Here, by calling in the aid of the senior boys, he was enabled to do as much justice to hundreds of children as he had before done to tens. 'In fact,' as he informs us himself, 'the children now came to me like flocks of sheep;' and in its best days the school was attended by a thousand children. The account of his position and

* Southey's "Life of Dr. Bell," vol. I.

character at this prosperous time, and of his relationships to his pupils, is very beautiful. Like all true teachers, he loved his work, and entered into it with his whole soul. Not content with instructing the children in school, he was their playmate in the intervals of lessons; in the evenings he had companies of them to tea, and on holidays he took bands of them on country excursions. No personal sacrifice seemed too great, if it helped him to increase his knowledge of his scholars, and to give him greater power of being useful to them. It would have been better for Lancaster, and for his ultimate reputation, if he had not been called from this scene of busy usefulness; but the report of the work he was doing began to spread, and crowds flocked to see what appeared like a miracle. One master with a thousand scholars! In the words of a biographer, 'Foreign princes, ambassadors, peers, commoners, ladies of distinction, bishops and archbishops,' turned their steps to the Borough Road,* and there they beheld a scene they were not likely to forget. The school presented a beautiful and orderly spectacle, Lancaster having the rare gift of inspiring his monitors and pupils with a spirit of enthusiasm and good order. The whole tone of the place

* Dunn's "Sketches."

was joyous, duties were agreeably varied from hour to hour, and though the noise often bewildered a visitor, it was at least the noise of animated work, and was succeeded in an instant, at the word of command, by perfect stillness.'* There was the little company of monitors, loyal to their master, full of zeal to please him, and proud of the beauty and fame of the spectacle in which they formed a part—all ranged round the school-room—each with a class of children. Let us pause to observe the lesson now going on in spelling. 'The scholars,' as Lancaster himself describes to us, 'have a desk before them with ledges on every side, and it is filled with sand to a level with these ledges; every boy is furnished with a sharp pointed wire to write, or more properly to print with. A word is then dictated by the monitor, for instance, "beer," and it is immediately sketched on the sand by every boy with the point of his skewer, and, when inspected by the monitor, another word is dictated as before. In this way, boys can write and spell a hundred words in the course of a morning, and five hundred boys can write and spell the same word at the same instant of time.'

This use of sand, which seems to have been confined to the younger classes, for teaching the

* Mr. Fitch in " Museum."

elements of spelling and arithmetic, was adopted from Dr. Bell's system; but it is right to remark that Lancaster came to prefer slates, both with junior and senior pupils.

The visitor passes on, and his attention is directed to a class engaged in reading; but, instead of the old-fashioned practice of each having book in hand, the children's eyes are all turned towards a reading-board or sheet hung on the wall, on which is printed in large type the lesson for the day—'a method,' exclaims Lancaster, 'whereby one book may serve for a whole school, instead of one child only. And observe the method employed. They read lines or sentences and paragraphs in rotation. They must read every word slowly and deliberately, pausing between each. They read long words in the same way, syllable by syllable; thus, in reading the word "composition," they would not read it at once, but by syllables, com-po-si-tion, making a pause at every syllable.' *

The lessons in arithmetic were conducted in a similar way, the old plan of setting sums to each pupil in a copy or on a slate, being superseded by the reading out of a question to a class—which then proceeded to work it out, the answer being called out at the close, and the errors checked—

* " Improvements in Education."

'a capital discovery,' cried a partizan in the "Edinburgh Review," 'for a boy can thus teach arithmetic without being acquainted with it himself—and everything else for that matter, for we see no one science which may not be taught in the same way. Every part of geometrical science may be taught by similar means, from the first proposition in Euclid to the sublime theorems of Newton and Laplace.' *

This pretension, quite Jacototian in its character, was, I am happy to say, not brought forward by Lancaster, but by his unwise friend the reviewer, and one regrets that the insinuation should be made against the poor man to the present day. Dr. Donaldson, in his "Lectures on Education," informs us that 'one of the most ingenious features of Lancaster's scheme was a plan by which boys, who did not know arithmetic at all, could teach it to others." (p. 60.) Lancaster's rule was that every monitor must be fully competent to teach the lessons of the class he was appointed to; and there was no exception made in the case of arithmetic, or any other subject.

So much for Lancaster's methods of teaching, by which reading, writing, and simple arithmetic were faithfully and correctly taught—a modest curriculum certainly, but one beyond which the

* November, 1810.

Committee of Council on Education did not for some years presume to go. If the visitor inquired into the secret of his discipline, he might have said, 'Friend, I have but one rule, "Let every child have at all times something to do, and a motive for doing it;"' and to do him justice this rule was well carried out in practice. But at the same time much of Lancaster's system of discipline was puerile and mischievous. The practice of giving rewards was carried to excess. 'It is no unusual thing for me,' he says, 'to deliver one or two hundred prizes at the same time, and at such times the countenances of the whole school exhibit a most pleasing scene of delight, as the boys who obtain prizes commonly walk round the room in procession, holding the prizes in their hands, and preceded by a herald proclaiming the fact before them. A collection of toys, bats, balls, pictures, kites, were suspended overhead, beaming glory and pleasure upon the school beneath.'

Again, in a corner of the school might be seen a boy sitting with a wooden log round his neck, from four to six pounds' weight. In aggravated cases it was customary to fasten the legs of offenders with wooden shackles, one or more, according to the offence, the shackle being a piece of wood from six inches to a foot long, tied to each leg ; and with these fetters the boy was ordered to walk round and round the schoolroom. And, by way of variety—for Lancaster was aware that 'familiarity breeds contempt,' even in punishments—a boy was occasionally put into a sack or basket, and hoisted to the ceiling in presence of all the rest, who laughed at the 'bird in the cage.' Boys who came to school with dirty faces had them washed before the whole school by little girls, who accompanied their ablutions with a gentle box on the ear. In justice to Lancaster, it must be stated that many of these absurd and injurious modes of penalty were invented to avoid flogging, which he held in great dislike ; and that latterly he came to discard many of them himself ; though one is much amused at seeing certain chapters in his tracts, headed 'Of logs,' 'of shackles,' ' of the basket,' ' of labels of disgrace.'

Before terminating this imaginary visit to Lancaster's school, it should be mentioned, to his credit, that within its walls he strove to enable his children to read the Bible, to understand its meaning, to love it, and to take it as the guide of their lives, at the same time studiously avoiding the introduction of controverted theological points, and everything peculiar to any sect or party, so that the religious prejudices of the parents might not be offended.* 'There is no saying,' observes Dr. Donaldson, 'that his method might not have gained the approbation of the whole nation had he not united religious instruction with it. All agreed that there should be religious instruction, but then who was to settle what that religious instruction should be?' Hence arose the sectarian storm referred to in the chapter on Dr. Bell, the cry of the 'Church in danger' having aroused from their apathy the 'whole bench of bishops.'

Lancaster's fortunes reached their zenith in 1805, when the king sent for him, and desired to have an account of his work. The interview is thus related by Corston, one of Lancaster's most faithful friends :—

'On entering the royal presence, the king said, "Lancaster, I have sent for you to give me an account of your system of education, which I hear has met with opposition. One master teach 500 children at the same time! How do you keep them in order, Lancaster?" Lancaster replied, "Please thy Majesty, by the same principle that thy Majesty's army is kept in order—by the word of command." His Majesty replied, "Good, good, it does not require an aged general to give the command; one of younger years can do it." Lancaster observed that in his schools the teach-

* " Museum."

ing branch was performed by youths, who acted as monitors. The king assented, and said, "Good." Lancaster then described his system, and he informed me that all present paid great attention, and were highly delighted; and as soon as he had finished, his Majesty said, "Lancaster, I highly approve of your system, and it is my wish that every poor child in my dominions should be taught to read the Bible; I will do anything you wish to promote this object."'

Royal subscriptions were given; the example was followed by many of the nobility, and, had Lancaster been discreet in the management of money, a career of honour and usefulness was open to him. But this public applause in a measure turned his head. Becoming impressed with the idea that he was, under Providence, destined to be the means of establishing a universal system of instruction, he published tract after tract in explanation of his system, and proceeded to deliver lectures in all the principal towns in the kingdom, illustrating his mode of teaching by help of monitors who accompanied him. In these journeys he occasionally met with discouragements, but oftener with honour and a cordial welcome; and during a single year he was able to say that a new school on his system had been opened every week.

He visited Ireland, also, and was the means of establishing a model school in Dublin, which was placed under the charge of a teacher of his own training. Money flowed in upon him, apparently in a perpetual stream. But this touched one of the weakest points in Lancaster's character. Instead of keeping a prudent reserve, he often spent this money recklessly in treats and presents to his scholars—thus, writing on one occasion from the country, in view of his own birthday, he said, 'I wish all my children to have a plum pudding and roast beef; do order it, and spend a happy evening with them.' In the fulness of his enthusiasm, also, and fired, perhaps, by the success of Fellenberg, he attempted to extend the monitorial system to agriculture, for which purpose a large piece of waste land was placed at his disposal by the Duke of Somerset. The boys who broke up the land were divided into classes, as in school, each under the charge of a monitor; everything was done by word of command; at the order, 'prepare to dig,' each spade was grounded and a foot placed upon it; at the word 'dig,' the spade was pressed into the soil, and on the order 'turn,' every spade was turned and the earth broken. It is needless to state that this scheme proved an utter failure—in fact, Lancaster's affairs soon became irretrievably involved; and the Borough Road school seemed likely to sink into ruin, when, in 1808, some benevolent gentlemen came forward, paid his debts, and resolved themselves into a committee, under the title of the Royal Lancasterian Institution, a name which was, in 1814, changed into that of the British and Foreign School Society. But this did not put an end to Lancaster's troubles. Though the society treated him handsomely, and allowed him an ample salary, they found that he would not work well in harness. They insisted on a correct statement of the income and expenditure of the school; but Lancaster looked upon this businesslike proceeding as intolerable interference, and one by one he quarrelled with them all, betook himself finally in anger to Tooting, where he commenced a private boarding-school, became more deeply involved, and at length emigrated to America in 1818. There his career was most chequered and sad; teaching and lecturing by turns, at times in affluent circumstances, and at others pinched by poverty, he passed on his unstable and fitful course, and finally died in 1838 from the effects of an accident in the streets of New York.

The student, who peruses Lancaster's pamphlets, 'will look almost in vain for guidance as to the best *methods* of teaching, or as to the right mode of presenting truth to a learner's mind'; but the impetus which he gave to popular education was incalculable; and he is in consequence fairly entitled to an honoured place in the history of education.* Mr. Fitch, for many years connected with the Borough Road College, estimates Lancaster's greatest work in the world to have been 'his vindication of a Christian and yet unsectarian system of education.' It was his desire, as we have seen, that every child in his school should be enabled to read and understand the Bible, but at the same time, he carefully abstained from associating religion with any sect or party. This scheme was not a trick to secure the support of all parties, but 'it grew out of the experience of a devout and earnest man, who, loving his own form of worship with passionate zeal, loved Christianity and the interests of children more earnestly still.'

   * Interesting memorials of Lancaster are preserved at the Borough Road College, several of his monitors' silver badges and medals being suspended in the Committee Room, and an adjoining street has just been re-named in honour of him.

SAMUEL WILDERSPIN.

Origin of Infant Schools—New Lanark Infant School the first—Others Established in London—Wilderspin appointed Master—First Experiences—Great Success—Organisation of Infant Schools—The First Infant Mistress—Wilderspin in Scotland—Status of the Scottish Teacher—What an Infant Teacher should be—His Five Rules—Teacher should follow Nature—The Child's Observing Powers—The "Kindergarten" System—Pictures. Recommended—Amusement with Instruction.

THE credit of having been the first to originate an infant school is generally given to Oberlin, the pastor of Waldbach, in Alsace, who, among the many marvellous acts of philanthropy by which his life was distinguished, conceived the happy idea of gathering together the children of his parishioners for combined amusement and instruction, while their parents were engaged at their daily avocations. This was about the close of the past century; and, about the beginning of the present, the same idea occurred to Robert Owen, who, in order to keep the children of his workers at the New Lanark Mills out of mischief and of danger, caused them to be gathered into a large apartment, where they were partly fed and taught by several women, under the superintendence of a Mr. James Buchanan, the first infant master, whose name is on record.* This was the first infant school in Great Britain, and the plan was found to be so beneficial, that several noblemen and gentlemen, among whom were Lord Brougham and the Marquis of Lansdowne, resolved to establish a similar school in London, which they did at Brewer's Green, Westminster. This was the first infant school in England, and according to the evidence of the then Lord Chancellor, before a House of Commons Committee in 1834, was the first complete infant school in the world.

'The first infant school in this island, I believe in the world,' said his lordship, 'was the one at Brewer's Green—Robert Owen's and Mr. Fellenberg's, which gave the idea, having both been formed in connection with an establishment manufacturing or agricultural, and so necessarily confined in their application; ours being everyday schools, where the children are neither fed, nor in any way helped, except by instruction

* Wilderspin's "Infant Education," p. 67.

and training.'* Mr. Buchanan was taken from New Lanark, to become master of the school at Brewer's Green; and an acquaintanceship, which he formed with Samuel Wilderspin, ended in the latter relinquishing his business pursuits, and taking charge of a similar, but more commodious establishment, opened in Spitalfields, in 1820. The term 'asylum' had been the name applied to Oberlin's and Owen's institutions, and this term is still, I believe, retained in France; but Wilderspin suggested the happier title of infant school, and advised that it should be confined to children from the ages of two to seven. He was naturally fond of children, and longed to do them good; but, being without experience and training in the management of numbers, the first difficulties he encountered were somewhat amusing. The following is an account, in his own words, of one of his earliest school days.

'When the mothers had left, a few of the children, who had been previously at a dame school, sat quietly; but the rest, missing their parents, crowded about the door. One little fellow, finding he could not open it, set up a loud cry of "Mammy, mammy!" and in raising this *delightful* sound, all the rest sim-

* Bartley's " Schools for the People," p. 108.

ultaneously joined. My wife, who, though reluctant at first, had determined, on my accepting the situation, to give me her utmost aid, tried with myself to calm the tumult; but our efforts were utterly in vain. The paroxysm of sorrow increased instead of subsiding, and so intolerable did it become, that she could endure it no longer, and left the room; and at length, exhausted by effort, anxiety, and noise, I was compelled to follow her example, leaving my unfortunate pupils in one dense mass, crying, yelling, and kicking against the door.'

'I will not attempt to describe my feelings; but, ruminating on what I then considered egregious folly in supposing that any two persons could manage so large a number of infants, I was struck by the sight of a cap of my wife's, adorned with coloured ribbon, lying on the table; and observing from the window a clothes-prop, it occurred to me that I might put the cap upon it, return to the school, and try the effect. The confusion when I entered was tremendous; but on raising the pole surmounted by the cap, all the children, to my great satisfaction, were instantly silent, and when any hapless wight seemed disposed to renew the noise, a few shakes of the prop restored tranquillity, and perhaps produced a laugh. The same thing, however, will not do long; the charms of this *wonderful* instrument, therefore, soon vanished, and there would have been a sad relapse, but for the marchings, gambols, and antics, I found it necessary to adopt, and which at last brought the hour of twelve, to my greater joy than can easily be conceived.

'Revolving these circumstances, I felt that that memorable morning had not passed in vain. I had, in fact, found the clue. It was now evident that the senses of the children must be engaged, that the great secret of training them was to descend to their level, and become a child; and that the error had been to expect in infancy what is only the product of after years.' *

The hint thus given led to his adoption of *appropriate action* as an accompaniment of infant lessons, a principle which is now largely carried out in all good infant schools. Wilderspin certainly followed to perfection the advice given by Abbott, that a teacher should make a study of his profession, and found himself inventing or trying, week by week, and day by day, some new school method, to enumerate all of which would only be to repeat what may be seen at the present time in the highly cultivated system of infant methods, in which interest and amusement pervade everything said or done. His

* "Early Discipline Illustrated," pp. 3, 4.

enthusiasm and knack as a teacher were not without their reward. His school became so popular that, though it was situated in one of the lowest and most obscure parts of the metropolis, the parents sent their children without solicitation; public attention was drawn to it, and visitors from all parts flocked to see the pleasing novelty, Wilderspin recording, with pardonable vanity, that 'it was no uncommon thing for several carriages to be seen standing at the door.' One of the early fruits of his success was the formation of the London Infant School Society, in 1824, and the establishment of infant schools in various parts of the country. Wilderspin was called from his duties as a teacher, and requested to lecture and found schools in the metropolis and elsewhere. The work which he did in this line fairly entitles him to be styled, 'organiser-in-chief of infant schools in Great Britain.' An account of his visits to the chief towns of England, Scotland, and Ireland—a most interesting and amusing narrative—was published by him under the title of "Early Discipline Illustrated"; and from this I quote freely in this paper, as well as from his other important work entitled "Infant Education."

Mrs. Wilderspin, whom he lovingly designates

'the first infant schoolmistress,' and who seems to have had as much faith in her husband as Madame Pestalozzi had in hers, with the additional merit of being a helpmate to him in his scholastic duties, entered upon charge of the school in his absence, and with unwearied patience and assiduity, kept the 200 children at their daily tasks, with no assistance save that of a daughter, then a child. The narrative of her labours has a touching end. Worn out by her exertions, the 'infant's friend' succumbed, and amid the tears of a thousand parents and children, who crowded the streets to pay respect to her memory, she was laid in the grave only four years after they had come as strangers to the neighbourhood, when many of the mourners had loaded them with insult and derision, and even pelted them with mud.

The shock nearly terminated Wilderspin's own existence; but after a dangerous and lengthened illness he was spared to be the agent in opening the schools referred to. It may be interesting to mention that David Stow, founder of Normal Schools, was the first to invite Wilderspin to Scotland, an invitation which he readily accepted, though the journey from London to Glasgow, which he made on horseback, occupied eight days, and was not unaccompanied by danger. He laboured for several weeks in getting the Drygate School, the first infant school in this city, into order, and relates how nearly the use of the ball frame had brought both himself and the school into disrepute. A fond mother happened to ask her child on his returning home, 'Weel, Sandy, what hae ye been at?' to which Sandy as naturally replied, 'Eh, mither, we've been countin' the beads.' The mother's native horror of popery was aroused, the alarm spread like fire, and, but for opportune explanation, the school would have been entirely deserted.

At the end of a month, these little ragamuffins were publicly examined in the Gaelic Chapel, at the west end of the city,* and about a mile from the Drygate. The children, who were from eighteen months to six years of age, and were unable to walk so far, were conveyed in carts, adorned with green boughs, guarded on each side by the Glasgow police, and followed by crowds of people. Inside of the church the audience numbered about 1,000, and, in their presence, questions on 'form, size, and position' were put and answered. A gentleman asked whether the chandelier was suspended or supported, and on a correct answer being made, he asked them to tell him the difference, whereupon a little boy

* Presumed to be St. Columba Church, Ingram Street, the site of the British Linen Company's Bank.

took from his pocket a piece of string, at the end of which was a button; placing the button on the palm of his hand, he answered, 'That is supported,' and holding the end of the string, so as to let the button fall, he said, 'That is suspended.' (If Mr. Stow was present, he must have been delighted at this juvenile example of 'picturing out.') The interrogator, after various questions, wished the children to mention something, not previously named, which was perpendicular, when, after a brief pause, a little black-eyed boy, whose head had been resting on his hand, shouted out, 'Ye're ane yersel.' The effect of this was so ludicrous, as to disconcert the questioner for a little, but soon rallying, he said, 'Suppose I were to strike Mr. Wilderspin, and knock him down, would he be perpendicular *then?*'—'No, he'd be horizontal,' was the prompt reply.

Some time after this, a class of children was taken to Paisley, Greenock, Rothesay, Edinburgh, and other places, which led to the beneficial results mentioned in the following chapter on Stow, whose biographer keeps Wilderspin's co-operation and success very much in the background. Wilderspin travelled over the greater part of the country to Aberdeen, Inverness, and Dingwall, and had numerous opportunities of observing the manners and customs of the people. One of those he noticed has, happily, no existence now, or exists only in benighted districts, and that is, a decided prejudice against *female* teachers, to whom parents, he says, could not be persuaded to send their children on any account; and to schools presided over by a master and mistress they would only send them on the understanding that the former was to perform the intellectual part, while the latter was to attend to the maternal department of morals and manners. Wilderspin's own opinion was, that women are not so fit as men to be conductors of infant schools, and that there should be in every school a master and a mistress—a mode of organisation which now prevails in every mixed school.

Since Wilderspin's time, women have come to be employed more and more in the work of teaching; and in infant and elementary work they seem likely to supersede men altogether. With all deference to his views, might we not adduce the great success of his wife and daughter in the conducting of the Spitalfields School while he was absent in the provinces, as a weighty argument against him? He noticed, with gratification, the superior standing of the Scottish schoolmaster to that of his own countrymen.

Whereas, in England, his position was far from being respectable, and was in some cases humiliating, in Scotland he was treated with respect, was received into the best society, was held next in estimation to the minister, and had generally a vacation of two months in duration, during which he could repair to the sea-shore, and recruit the health and strength necessary for the discharge of his important and responsible duties.*

The germs of Stow's training system are undoubtedly to be found in the pages of Wilderspin, *e. g.*, Wilderspin remarks, 'The first thing we attempt to do in an infant school is to set the children thinking, to get them to examine, compare, and judge of all those matters which their dawning intellects are capable of mastering.'† And again, 'As the fundamental principle of the system, I would say *Let the children think for themselves.* If they arrive at erroneous conclusions, assist them in attaining the truth, but let them with such assistance arrive at the truth by their own exertions. Little good would be done if you should say to a child, " *That* is wrong, *this* is right," unless you enable the child to perceive wherein the error of the one and the truth of the other consist.' (p. 147.)

* " Early Discipline," p. 117.
† " Infant Education," p. 146.

This method, of course, dates as far back as the time of Socrates, whose dialogues afford copious illustration of this mode of teaching.

Like Stow, Wilderspin is strongly in favour of the mixed system, remarking that in his experience, little girls shew more susceptibility and kindness, and excel in all that relates to the affections, while boys are not so soon excited, but are far more energetic. The influence of the one sex on the other cannot but be highly beneficial. When associated, opportunities occur for the exhibition of their peculiar characters, and the invigorating of their respective feelings. 'I never knew a little girl,' he says, 'fall on the playground, without a little boy helping her up; or a little boy hurt himself without some little girl or girls running to soothe and assist him.' (p. 105.)

In regard to the moral training of the playground, the views of the two men coincide in a striking way. After remarking that for purposes of health the playground is an invaluable adjunct to every school, and that fruit trees and flowers should be planted in it, to train the children to honesty and to cultivate their taste, Wilderspin says, 'It is there the child shews itself in its true character, and thereby gives the master an opportunity of nipping in the bud its evil propensities'; and again, 'For the purpose of observation, the playground will afford an admirable opportunity, and it is on this account, as well as that it affords exercise and amusement to the children, a most indispensable appendage to an infant school. It is here the child will shew its character in a true light. The playground may be compared to the world, where the little children are left to themselves, and where it may be seen what effects their education has produced; for if they are fond of fighting and quarrelling, it is there that they will do it; if they are artful, it is there they will seek to practise their cunning, and this will give the master an opportunity of applying the proper remedy; whereas, if kept in school (which they must be if there be no playground), these evil inclinations will never manifest themselves until they get into the street, and consequently the master will have no opportunity of attempting a cure. I have seen many children who behaved very orderly in the school, but the moment they got into the playground they manifested the principle of self-love to such a degree that they would wish all the rest of the children to be subservient to them, and on these refusing to let them bear rule, would begin to use force, in order to compel them to comply. This is conduct that ought to be checked, and what time so proper as the first stages of infancy?' (pp. 139, 140.)

Both authors agree as to the object for which they were desirous to see the blessings of education widely diffused—viz., the moral training of the children of the poor. Both coincide in thinking that a great deal of the crime and misery existing in this country might be decreased by means of early moral training. In this respect they evince a spirit similar to that of Pestalozzi.

In regard to the qualifications of infant teachers, Wilderspin is of opinion that the virtues of 'patience, gentleness, perseverance, self-possession, energy, knowledge of human nature, and, above all, piety, are requisite to ensure success.' Indeed, he says, we cannot be too circumspect in the choice of the persons to whom we commit the care and education of the rising generation. For the guidance of teachers he proposes the following five short rules, which experience had recommended to himself:—

I. Never to correct a child in anger.

II. Never to deprive a child of anything without returning it again.

III. Never to break a promise.

IV. Never to overlook a fault.

V. In all things to set before the children an example worthy of imitation. (p. 106.)

In another place he says, 'The first grand object of the master and mistress of an infant school is to win the love of the children by banishing all slavish fear. One kind action influences a child more than a volume of words. The fundamental principle of the infant school system is love.'

He makes no inconsiderable contribution to the science of education when he says, 'The art of education is to follow nature, to assist and imitate her in her way of rearing men. The ancient inhabitants of the Baleares followed nature in the manner of teaching their children to be good archers, when they hung their dinner aloft by a thread, and left them to bring it down by their skill in archery.'

He is at one with Pestalozzi in insisting that a knowledge of things should precede a knowledge of words; let the children examine into and find out the nature and properties of objects, and there is no fear of their remaining ignorant of their names. 'One of the teacher's duties, then, should be to excite a spirit of inquiry in the child, to foster that inquisitive spirit which is so natural to young children; and, having excited a spirit of inquiry, you should next endeavour to direct it to proper objects—such objects as are suited for investigation by its infantile faculties;

these, of course, will be things which have relation to its animal senses; the nature and properties of bodies, ascertainable by the application of those senses, &c. Having induced it to examine for itself, you are now to elicit the ideas excited by each object respectively; ascertain the child's notion on the subject, and having thus brought it to put its ideas into a definitive shape in language; having taught it to use its reason and judgment freely, and to express its notions fearlessly and candidly—it matters not how simple the subject—you are to attempt the correction of its erroneous notions, by putting forth your own, in as simple a way as possible—not so as to induce the child to give up its own opinions and adopt yours in their place, but in such a way as to direct its reasoning process to the attainment of truth; to induce a comparison and consequent discovery of its own error.' (p. 149.)

Suitable exercise for the observing powers of children is afforded by the lessons on weight, form, number, and colour given after the manner of Froebel in his Kindergarten system, which should be studied by every infant teacher in supplement to that of Wilderspin and others. The fields and hedges around every country school afford abundant material in their wealth of plants and flowers for enabling the skilful teacher to cultivate the observing faculties of her children; in fact, as may be fully perceived by the perusal of " On the Culture of the Observing Powers of Children," by Miss Youmans, botany yields to no other science in the facilities it affords in this department. The encouragement held out by the Education Department, in the shape of ample pecuniary grants to infant schools, should make it an easy matter for school managers to have their schools abundantly furnished with objects, specimens, and pictorial illustrations.

In respect to methods of teaching, Wilderspin, as before mentioned, was the inventor of the ball-frame, and is a strong advocate for the teaching of numbers from the concrete to the abstract. He gives excellent advice on the teaching of infants by means of pictures, whether' of Scripture incidents, or of natural history, or of trades and manufactures; thus, when a Bible story, such as the raising of Lazarus from the dead, is the subject of lesson, a picture of the same should be suspended in view of the children. The series of pictures which Wilderspin used was twenty-four in number; a variety was afforded by the children being required at times to find out the pictures that indicated various incidents, which the teacher named, such as 'point out the picture of the Nativity of Jesus Christ': the children were always delighted with this mode of teaching, and would of their own accord crave information on a new picture, and thus a desire to read the Bible for themselves was early and strongly implanted in their minds. Wilderspin cautions the teacher against exposing all his pictures to view at once and at all times; for, in this case, 'familiarity breeds contempt.' The pictures should be brought to view only when required as subjects for the daily lesson. He also recommends the adoption of object-lesson cards, such as are in general use at the present time, and which, coupled with a small cabinet of objects, are of great service in enabling the child to understand what it reads in the ordinary lesson book.

Wilderspin's whole system is a combination of amusement with instruction. 'Make your system interesting, lively, and inspiriting, and your scholars will neither be able nor willing to slumber over it.' The principle is carried to an absurd extent in the rhyming lessons on weights and measures, &c.—

> ' Two pints will make one quart,
> Four quarts one gallon strong;
> Some drink but little, some too much,
> To drink too much is wrong.'

And the stanza in wine, oil, and spirit measure :—

> 'A little wine within
> Oft cheers the mind that's sad;
> But too much brandy, rum, or gin
> No doubt is very bad.'

A knowledge of weights and measures is better taught by having specimens of these in view of the children when lessons involving their use are being given.

This and other defects in teaching became magnified under teachers who had no training, and but limited experience; so that the advocates and promoters of infant schools throughout the country soon became painfully aware that something more must be done than opening schools and providing teachers, if their influence for good was to meet public expectation. This led to the starting of an institution for training teachers, as the only way of really improving the infant schools in the country, and to the formation of the Home and Colonial Infant School Society in 1836.

Wilderspin may be classed among the many educationists who
> 'Omnes illacrimabiles
> Urguentur ignotique longâ
> Nocte, carent quia vate sacro.'*

No one, as far as I am aware, has written a

* Horace, Odes IV. 9.

biographical notice of him; and the dates of his birth and of his death are consequently unknown; but, after perusing his works, I am of opinion that the name of this patriarch of infant teaching, who struck the proper key-note in infant education, and whose wonderful enthusiasm and energy gave an impetus to the foundation of numerous schools in this country, should not be allowed to go down to oblivion.*

* James Simpson, author of a work on "Popular Education," and convener of the Edinburgh Infant School Society, passes the following eulogy on Wilderspin, 'I feel it not only a duty but a delight to devote a note to this singularly meritorious individual, whom it concerns the public to know, before they are called upon, as they *must* be, to approve of his receiving a national tribute for the benefits he has conferred on his fellow-men, the toils he has cheerfully endured, the pittance he has generally conditioned as bare livelihood, and last, but not least, the obstructions and persecutions with which his enlightened and benevolent labours have been met. If an infant school is to be organized in the extreme north of Scotland, Mr. Wilderspin will come from Cheltenham where he resides, for the humblest travelling expenses and means of subsistence, and devote six weeks to the training of the pupils and teachers, while by his lectures and zeal he never fails to give such an impetus to the whole region which he visits, as often gives him several schools to set agoing before he is called elsewhere; he is ready for any infant educational enterprise to the sacrifice of every selfish consideration, and once offered himself to go to the West Indies to organize schools for the children of the negroes, if he should perish in the attempt.' (p. 149.)

DAVID STOW.

Sabbath School Teaching—Experience in the Saltmarket—Opens a Model School—The First Normal School—Its Early Working—Criticism Lessons—Bible Teaching—Owen's Visit—Second Normal School—The " Training" System—Visit to England—A " Training Lesson "—Picturing Out—Bible Lesson " Pictured Out"—Sympathy of Numbers—The " Mixed" System—Results in America—The Gallery and Playground—His Influence on Education.

DAVID STOW, one of the few original educationists whom Scotland has produced, and whose name is associated with the institution of training colleges for teachers, was born at Paisley, in 1793. He came of a very respectable family, and was contemporary with one or two well known natives of the place, among whom were Professor Wilson (the 'Christopher North' of "Blackwood's Magazine"), and the poet Tannahill. Having received his early education at Paisley Grammar School, he became connected in 1811 with a large commercial house in Glasgow. Though the best society in that city was open to him, he preferred to devote his leisure time to the instruction of the poor, in his self-denying love and labour for whom he may be fairly likened to Pestalozzi. Stow's life is indeed a wonderful example of what an ordinary citizen, not trained to teaching, or deriving any pecuniary advantage from his educational efforts, can do towards spreading the blessings of education.

In reading the memoir of his life, one is struck by the similarity of the experience, that turned his attention to teaching, and that of Robert Raikes, originator of Sabbath Schools. Having to pass daily through the Saltmarket, his spirit was roused within him at the misery, ignorance, and vice which he witnessed, and he earnestly longed to do something which might help to overcome these evils. A short experience taught him that it would be useless to attempt a reformation of the *old*, and he accordingly resolved to try his first experiment upon the *young*. This experiment was in the field of Sabbath school teaching. Having hired a room in the Saltmarket, he began what he called his 'deep sea fishing' among the poorest families in the neighbourhood, inviting the children to meet him on the following Sabbath. Twenty-eight boys and girls, of ages varying from eight to fourteen years, responded to the call, of whom five only could tell the name of the *first man*, or that there had been a first man.* They were at the same time as unruly a set of children as could well be imagined, and his first experiences, as related by his biographer, were sufficiently discouraging.

'On the night of his opening his school, in his selected locality, he encountered much rudeness. No sooner was the class arranged, and had prayer begun, than the lights were extinguished. When rekindled, Mr. Stow was alone, the class had escaped. He cheerfully resumed his visiting of every family, and without uttering a single complaint, he won back all his pupils, and secured obedience.

'A bold and restless boy, ragged and barefooted, had entered the class; lines, the shadows of cunning, were already traced on a naturally frank and open countenance. Placed on the third seat from the front, the temptation was great, and he yielded to it; having ingeniously taken hold of a large pin with his toes, he darted it against the bare feet and legs of as many as he could reach of those before him; they leaped yelling from their seats, and he stood in the midst of them, apparently alarmed by this unexpected turmoil.

* Stow's "Training System," 10th edit., p. 50.

'On discovering his conduct, Mr. Stow neither denounced nor expelled him, nor did he adopt the clumsy expedient of sending him to another seat; but he reasoned with him as to the pain he had thoughtlessly given to his classmates, and as to its continuance after his fun ended. He appealed to his sympathy, and won it. In the course of a short time he gave him charge of the candle lights—there was then no gas—and by no awkwardness in snuffing them were they ever afterwards extinguished. The boy became an enthusiastic scholar. Impatience in the teacher would have, in all likelihood, destroyed that boy's character.'*

In this small Sabbath school, which was opened in 1816, the leading principles of Stow's system of teaching were first practically developed. An experience of ten years' duration, however, brought him to the conclusion that the instruction given on the Sabbath-day was apt to be effaced by the evil influences of the other six days of the week, and to remedy this, he opened in 1826 a week-day moral training school, which he intended to be a model establishment for others of the kind in the city and throughout the country. The building, which was situated in Drygate Street, was capable of accommodating about 100

* " Memoir of Stow," by the Rev. Dr. Fraser, p. 41.

pupils, and gave facilities for training a few students, male and female, who were meant to extend the new educational system to country districts and villages, but chiefly in the larger towns. One or two infant schools had shortly before this been established in London, and to the most important of these, taught by Mr. Wilderspin, Mr. Stow paid a personal and observant visit. At his suggestion, Mr. Wilderspin came to Scotland and delivered some lectures in Glasgow and Edinburgh, which were of great service to the cause of infant education.

The Glasgow Education Society also, with whom Mr. Stow was associated, being desirous to spread a knowledge of the modes of teaching practised under his auspices, adopted Lancaster's plan, and sent a class of children, accompanied by a master and mistress, to visit different towns and villages; and, in several instances, such an impression was produced, that schools on the training system were at once established.* An educational society was originated in Edinburgh, and, in compliance with an invitation, the model class set out, in 1829, on what was then a long and fatiguing journey by stage-coach, and received in the capital a cordial and flattering welcome, being exhibited before admiring audi-

* "Memoir," p. 88.

ences in the Waterloo Rooms, for three successive days. This led to the establishment of the Edinburgh Model Infant School, and to the awakening of public attention to the subject of elementary education.

One of the grandest results of the public interest thus excited, was the establishment of a Normal school for the training of teachers in the most approved methods of teaching, to which the Drygate School, and a juvenile school in the parish of St. John's, which Mr. Stow had subsequently opened, were both transferred. The foundation-stone of this institution, which is now known under the name of the Glasgow Church of Scotland Normal School, and is situated in Dundas Vale, New City Road, was laid on 14th November, 1836, and the building was finished in its present complete state in 1838. The cost of the site and building was £15,700, of which the Committee of Council on Education granted nearly two-thirds—viz., £9,500. The institution stands within an area of about an acre, the vacant space being laid out in flower-plots and play-grounds for the students and children. Of this institution Mr. Stow was for several years the presiding genius, his system of training being carried out both in the instruction of the children and in the preparation of the students for the vocation of teachers. Now was fulfilled the great desire he had cherished for years. The schoolmaster could now be trained to his calling, as the mechanic, the sailor, the soldier, and the lawyer had formerly been; the candidate-teacher could see a proper system of teaching in practice; he could have it explained to him by suitable trainers; and, most important of all, he could put his own hand to the work, and become skilled in the art. That former state of things had passed away in which the teacher had been left to train himself, and had no model school to look at, far less a Normal institution to be trained in.*

The number of students received into training during the earlier years was, of course, limited, seldom exceeding forty to fifty, while an attendance of three months only was required. It was not till 1855 that a two years' course was introduced, under the auspices of the Committee of Council, and it was nearly ten years later before this course was made compulsory. Students of both sexes were received from the beginning, and while the proportion of males to females is now generally about equal, such was not the case at first, for I find that in 1836 the proportion was ten to one. In reference to

* 'Training System," p. 10.

the means adopted for the professional training of the students, I make the following quotation from Dr. Fraser, who was himself a student :—

'In the working of the institution Mr. Stow introduced two methods of culture, which had the best possible effect in giving the students a kindlier interest in one another, and in revealing whatever excellencies might be possessed by them. The one method was "private criticisms," and the other, "public lessons," given weekly. Both were regulated by Mr. Stow himself.

'In the first or "private criticisms" the students were seated in their gallery, and answered as children, while, in succession, their fellow-students gave them lessons in reading, spelling, arithmetic, or catechetical exercises, under the guidance of Mr. Stow and the Rector. The "criticism" was given during the lesson; manner, matter, look, intonation, forms of questions, were all referred to, exhibited, corrected with gentleness, and always most effectively. The females gave lessons in a separate hall, and were similarly criticised and guided.

'The second method of practical culture was a somewhat severe but beneficial ordeal; the resources of every student were taxed by it to the very utmost; to the ambitious and energetic it gave the best outlet for distinction, and to the timid confidence. There was, perhaps, no part of the training of the students more attractive to a stranger, when permitted to enjoy a privilege which, for obvious reasons, was rarely granted, than the public "criticism lessons." The plan originated by Mr. Stow was so controlled by him as to prove most effective. But for his firmness and kindly bearing it might have been the source of irritating personal rivalry. To four students a lesson each was prescribed a week before it was required, that it might be carefully prepared. The four lessons generally embraced a Scripture narrative or emblem; an object; reading, with explanations; and a fact or law in science. When the children were seated in the gallery, and the students had assembled in their presence, each of the four students in his turn gave his lesson, ten or twelve minutes being allowed; and the teachers noted not only every defect in pronunciation, in manner, in the arrangement of the lessons, in the ellipses formed, or in the method of questioning, but also all that was commendable. It was a trying time; but these respective exercises gave the student greater confidence and ease in the subsequent management of his own school, and constrained each to study the lessons given, and to try the best means of rivetting attention. No suggestions were made in the presence of the scholars. The students, the head-masters of the departments, the Rector, and Mr. Stow adjourned to the students' hall, when, Mr. Stow or the Rector presiding, the four who had given lessons on the preceding week, and had been criticised, began, in turn, the review of the lessons given, and spoke for a limited time. Others followed. No one who has listened to the lessons and the subsequent criticisms can have forgotten the frank, off-hand, hearty commendation, the gentle rebukes, the sometimes subtle and sometimes broad humour of the more experienced critics, and the timid, half-hesitating remarks of beginners. Sometimes the lessons were analysed, and discussion sustained in such a way as to show how deeply some of the teachers were inquiring into the philosophy of education, and making the human mind their study. They were thus taught to speak accurately, and with ease; to observe closely, to treat each other as gentlemen, and to think. To no part of Mr. Stow's labours, in the practical training of teachers, is greater importance to be attached than to this. It contributed greatly to the subsequent efficiency of the schoolmaster, and diffused a higher "*esprit de corps.*"' (pp. 156-159).

The system of criticism lessons thus described is still carried on, and is pre-eminently useful for the purposes of training, and calling attention to principles. The practice of private criticism, adopted by Mr. Stow, is, however, in my opinion, liable to many objections, and I think the custom, now adopted, of introducing a class of children at all the criticism lessons is much to be preferred. When the children retire from the room, the students criticise the various lessons freely, pointing out in what respect each teacher has departed from recognised principles. In giving the lessons the students are instructed to keep in view two very important objects—first, to train the observing powers of the children, and second, to convey some useful knowledge. Many of the lessons thus given afford excellent specimens of how useful information, on common objects, can be presented to children in a very attractive form.

The great feature of Mr. Stow's institution was the Bible teaching, which attracted visitors from all parts. Among others, came the celebrated Robert Owen, 'the well-known Socialist Reformer,' and the originator in Great Britain of infant schools, the promoters of the London schools above mentioned having taken their model from his. On Owen's mind, according to Dr. Fraser, who relates the incident of his visit in a touching manner, a very serious impression was produced by the vivid word-painting of the Scripture-lesson given on the occasion by Mr. Stow himself. 'His features changed. At first listless, he became earnestly attentive. His whole aspect betokened deep emotion, and ere the lesson was closed, the tears coursed down his cheeks. What secret springs were touched, what deep sympathies were evoked, and pulsed for an instant through that man's soul, no one can tell. His impassive calmness soon returned; but he left with a sadder look and deeper thoughtfulness than when he came.' (p. 130.)

In consequence of circumstances that succeeded the Disruption, Mr. Stow was obliged to resign possession of this Institution to the General Assembly of the Church of Scotland, and on the 8th of May, 1845, he, along with his fellow-directors, the teachers, 50 students, and 700 children, marched out of the building, and founded the Glasgow Free Church Normal School in Cowcaddens, over which he continued to preside till the day of his death in 1864.

The two institutions, thus founded by his exertions, still flourish side by side, both doing valuable service in the training of teachers, and faithfully fulfilling the object for which they were established. The reader will excuse my having been so minute in giving the outline of Stow's life, because of its intrinsic interest, and of his being the founder of the venerable Institution of which I am Principal, and which, as I have stated, lays claim to being the first formally-instituted Training College in the United Kingdom.

Mr. Stow wrote many fugitive papers and several books on education, the chief of which is entitled the "Training System," which has run through many editions, the one from which I quote in these pages being the tenth, and published in 1854. This work, which embraces most of what Mr. Stow had previously written, illustrates fully the system of teaching which he spent a lifetime in bringing to perfection, and is well worthy of careful study.

The chief features of the system, the principles he insists on, may be comprehended under four or five heads, the first of which is—

Training, as opposed to *teaching, telling,* or *instructing.* The distinction between *teaching* and *training* is one which is by no means generally understood; but it is a distinction which teachers should clearly and fully comprehend. Solomon said, 'Train up a child in the way he should go, and when he is old he will not depart from it,' a precept which is still to be seen in conspicuous characters in the lobby of the Normal School, and in the students' hall. Two hundred years before Stow, John Locke had recommended 'the method of teaching children by repeated practice, and the same action done over and over again, under the eye and direction of the tutor, till they have got the habit of doing it well,' and Dr. Samuel Johnson had very pithily said, 'You cannot by all the lecturing in the world enable a man to make a shoe.' The principle of training, therefore, was by no means new; but Stow applied it so skilfully, so thoroughly, and so successfully in school work, that, in his hands and in his writings, the principle has the appearance of freshness and originality. His own remarks on the subject are very interesting.

'A child may be clumsy in his manners, or disorderly in his habits. For example, if instead of hanging up his cap on the proper nail or peg, he throws it on the floor—lift it who may —then cause the boy to lift it *himself*, and to place it calmly on the peg. *See* that he does this properly and instantly on receiving the command, and repeat the practical lesson until he acquires the habit of doing so of himself.

'If a child comes to school with dirty hands, should the master say to the child, "It is wrong to come to school so; you must wash them properly before you come here," this would be teaching. To make the inquiry audibly in the hearing of all, "How ought children to come to school?—ought their hands to be dirty or ... clean"? at the same time holding up the dirty hand, and comparing it with the clean hand of another child,—also causing him to wash his hand,—is training. The instruction, or teaching, may, or may not, be attended to; but the intellectual perception brought out by the contrast of the clean hand with the dirty one, along with the actual washing of it, and the sympathy of companionship, never fail, in any case, to produce the habit of cleanliness.

'A child may be told to make a bow on entering or leaving a room, and every plan of making it gracefully may have been fully laid before him; but, without training, he will make a pitiful exhibition on attempting his first obeisance. It is equally the same in carving a fowl—no teaching or lecturing will suffice without training or doing.

'A person destined for a public speaker may have read much, and been taught much—he may know most critically all the rules of elocution; but he will make a poor figure, unless he has applied himself practically to the art; until, in fact, he has been trained to public speaking.

'It is recorded of Dean Swift that he had often been *teaching* or telling his servant in vain to close the library door when she left the room. One day she entered her master's study, and requested permission of him that she might go a few miles into the country, to the marriage of a friend, which was granted. The door, as usual, was left open; annoyed at this, the Dean permitted the girl to leave the house several minutes, and then ordered another servant to follow, and to say to her that her master wished to speak with her. She reluctantly obeyed the summons, and returning in great haste inquired what her master wished to say. The Dean calmly replied, "Oh, nothing particular; shut the door." What *teaching* had failed to do, *training* in this instance fully accomplished—the door was ever afterwards properly closed.

'In intellectual teaching, a child may commit to memory the whole rules of English or Latin grammar, and may be able to repeat every example, and answer every query contained in the book itself, thoroughly and correctly; and thus far he shows the extent of his instruction or teaching. The child is only under training, however, when he is put to the work of applying these rules to the formation of a sentence in speaking or writing; and it is evident that the person well taught in the rules may be exceedingly ill trained, or not trained at all, to the practice of speaking or writing grammatically. Ere the child, therefore, is a trained grammarian, his mind must be made to bear upon the subject—he must understand it, and actually apply for himself the rules of speaking and writing correctly.

'In the moral department, storing the mind with Scripture texts is teaching or instruction—seeing that the child practically does the things as they are required in real life, renders the process training.' (pp. 78-80).

The distinction between teaching and training is still further brought out in Stow's observations on Bible training, on which he places great importance, the great object of his life having been the moral upbringing of the young; and, in course of time, the gradual amelioration of what he called the *sunken* and the *sinking* classes of society, which he estimated as constituting, at that period, *one half* of the population of Glasgow. (p. 88.)

The following are his definitions of Bible reading, Bible teaching, and Bible training :—

1. 'Bible reading we understand to be the simple reading of the words of Scripture, without

explanation or analysis, and is what is practised at the present day in five cases out of six. Thirty years ago it was all but universal. The whole meaning of a passage or text of Scripture frequently rests on one or two words. If these are not understood, the reader may with equal profit read the whole passage in a foreign tongue.

2. 'Bible teaching we understand to include an explanation or telling by the master of the meaning of what is read, instructing the child, as it is termed, and conveying the explanation in words more or less simple, which the pupil may, or may not comprehend, and which point the teacher does not use any systematic means of ascertaining. This explanation or questioning may be confined, as is too much the practice, to the mere facts, without the lesson itself, or it may include both. When questioning is added to telling or instruction, such an examination then forms one step in the process of training, but still rises no higher than examination.

3. 'Bible training is not simple reading, although the passage must be read or repeated. Nor is it mere telling or explanation, although the meaning must be told and explained, but not entirely by the master ; nor is it mere questioning by the master, and answering by the

scholars, *vivâ voce*, or what may be gathered from a printed book; and yet questions are put, and answers are received, but they are mixed with ellipses by a particular process, and in such a way, as that instead of the master-trainer drawing the lesson, the children are required and enabled to do so to him in their own language, more or less simple. The being able to do this is the proof that the whole subject-matter has been clearly pictured out, and rendered visible to the mind's eye of the children. What the children mentally see, they can therefore express in their own language. We may here remark that the theory and practice of Bible training proceed upon the principle, that nearly every passage of Scripture, when naturally pictured out in words, explains its own meaning.' (pp. 168, 169.)

The system first mentioned—viz., Bible reading—is almost worthless in its moral results; and of this fact Mr. Stow gives a melancholy though amusing instance, which fell under his own observation.

'A few years ago, I visited a school in one of the large towns of England, taught on the monitorial system, and was introduced to the master by one of the directors, who stated that he was a very superior teacher, and had his boys, to the number of at least 350, in good order. I found the school, as stated, in excellent order, all busy at spelling lessons or reading the Scriptures. On reaching the highest class, in company with the master and director, I asked the former if he ever questioned the scholars on what they read. He answered, "No, sir, I have no time for that; but you may, if you please." I answered that, except when personally known to the teacher, I never questioned children in any school. "By all means, do so now if you please; but *them* thick-headed boys cannot understand a word, I am sure." Being again asked to put a few questions, I proceeded: "Boys, show me where you are reading," and to do them justice, they read fluently. The subject was the story of Eli and his two sons. I caused the whole of them to read the first verse—"And Eli had two sons, Hophni and Phinehas." "Now, children, close your books," (presuming it impossible that any error could be committed in such a plain narrative, I proceeded), "Well, who was Eli?" *No answer.* This question appeared too high, requiring an exercise of thought, and a knowledge not to be found in the verse read. I therefore descended in the scale and proceeded, "Tell me how many sons Eli had?"—"Ugh?" "Had Eli any sons?"—"Sir?" "Open your books, if you please, and read again." Three or four read in succession, "And Eli had two sons, Hophni and Phinehas." "Now, answer me, boys; how many sons had Eli?"—"Soor?" "Who do you think Eli was? Had Eli any sons?"—"Ugh?" "Was he a man, do you think, or a bird, or a beast? Who do you think Eli was, children?"—"Soor?" "Look at me, children, and answer me this—If Eli had two sons, do you think his two sons had a father?"—"Soor?" "Think, if you please, had Eli ANY sons?" *No answer.* "Well, since you cannot tell me how many sons Eli had, how many daughters had he, think you?"—"*Three*, sir." "Where do you find that, children?—look at your Bibles. Who told you that Eli had three daughters?" —"Ugh?" The director turned upon his heels, and the master said, "Now, sir, *didn't I tell you them fellows could not understand a word?*" This I term Scriptural *reading;* those who choose may term it Scriptural *education.*' (pp. 118, 119.)

On Bible *training*, Mr. Stow bestows the following panegyric: 'We are aware that no treatise can exhibit the power and beauty of Bible training; for, in addition, it requires the sympathy of master and scholars, the eye, the action, and the tones of the voice. Indeed, to know the system properly, we must be able to practise it.' (p. 173.) And, again, he remarks—

'A Bible training lesson so thoroughly brings out the true meaning of the passage, and so enlarges the mind by analysing the natural picture on which the moral or spiritual lessons rest, that we promise the trainer or conductor, high as his knowledge of Scripture truth may be, as great an increase to his own mind, as he communicates to any or all of his pupils. Oftentimes have I commenced a lesson with my Sabbath pupils, thinking I knew the subject pretty fully, but ere I was done, the observations or answers of my scholars on the subject-matter of the lesson, threw a flood of light on the whole subject, removing perhaps a difficulty, or an apparent contradiction, and rendering the lesson to be drawn from the natural picture apparent as noon-day—a training lesson thus becoming a practical commentary. We promise every Bible trainer, therefore, a rich addition to his previous stock of knowledge, and, what is of more importance, an increased facility in acquiring it; his own mind, as well as his pupils', being gradually sharpened and improved.' (p. 180.)

As an example of the method to be pursued, he instances a passage of Scripture which 'is generally considered above the comprehension of children, but which may be rendered comparatively easy of solution,' viz.:—

'As the hart panteth after the water-brooks, so panteth my soul after thee, O God.' (Psalm xlii, 1).

On the training system, the teacher should first get the children to understand the natural picture given by the Psalmist, by giving a short outline of the habits of the hart,—' its panting—what is panting—why it pants—nature of the climate—dust—heat—being hunted it may be on the dry mountains of Judea—whether it must have plunged into or drank from the water-brooks formerly, before it could long or pant after them, &c.' (p. 170). When the natural picture is thus made clear to their minds, the children will themselves be able to perceive the force of the analogy, ' So panteth my soul after thee, O God.'

In respect to religious teaching in school, he observes: 'The province of the schoolmaster, I conceive to lie in training in the elements of Divine truth, just as he trains, or ought to train, in the elements of any and of every secular branch of education which he is required or entrusted to teach. This he can best and most satisfactorily accomplish by analysing and picturing out Scripture in its emblems, precepts, history, &c., along with his pupils in a simple and natural manner.' (p. 16.)

But while Mr. Stow placed so much importance on Bible training, he was equally anxious that the training system should be carried out in teaching other branches; and in these days when there is a growing desire for science teaching in elementary schools, some useful hints may be gathered from Stow, who, as the following passage will testify, entertained a sensible view of what elementary science teaching in schools ought to be. Having stated that the teaching of science by means of gallery lessons ought to form a distinct feature in schools, even for the children of the poor, and that those lessons should be given orally, and without a text book, he says,—

'The lessons during the first stage, or the outlines, at whatever age the child commences his course, ought to be exceedingly simple, and should comprehend a number of the more obvious things in nature and in art, which every child ought to know in their great outlines, before he is perplexed with minute points, or the use of technical terms; a knowledge of which he gradually acquires, as he advances from stage to stage.

'As a child, I wish to know what wheaten bread and oaten bread are; the distinction in quality, and how they are made; how butter and cheese are made; what salt is; how wine is made, and of what composed; what brown and loaf sugars are; the nature of tea and coffee, with the places where they are produced, and how they are brought to the condition in which they are found when used at home at the fireside; the distinction between wool, cotton, flax, and silk, both how they are produced, and why more or less warm.

'The child ought to be made acquainted with articles of furniture. These are continually presented to his notice, and they afford the means of exercising his powers of observation and training him to think. Their nature and relative qualities ought to be made familiar to him.

'The natural history of the more common animals, domestic and foreign, is also an object of interest and a means of enlargement to the young mind, particularly when united with a short history, not merely of the habits of the animals themselves, but of the countries and inhabitants in and among which Providence has placed them, and the peculiar adaptation of each to its own particular circumstances. As a child, I wish to know why the swallow is not seen during winter; why the hen has open feet, and the duck webbed; with other more minute points of the formation of animals; why the butterfly is seen in the summer only; from what origin it has sprung. What are all these? the child naturally inquires, and whence do the wings of the latter derive their pearly whiteness? Of what use rats and mice are, seeing they are so troublesome in our dwellings, and why and when they may be killed without our being chargeable with cruelty; how the foot of the reindeer is suited to the frozen regions of Lapland, that of the horse to our own, and the camel's to the sandy deserts of Arabia. From each and all of these training lessons, the children may learn something of the power, and wisdom, and goodness of God to all His creatures; and such lessons should uniformly be drawn from the children by every trainer during the daily oral training lessons.

'The child sees himself surrounded on every side by men of trade and handicraft, and he wishes and ought to know, not merely the qualities of things, and the materials in use, but how they are moulded, or joined, or mixed, or decomposed, so as to render them serviceable. He sees the smith form a nail or a horse-shoe; why does he heat the iron in a furnace, before laying it on the anvil, and striking it with the hammer? The uses of the pulley, the screw, and the lever, ought to be pictured out to him by analogy and familiar illustrations. The child sees paper; why not woven as a piece of cloth, and why more or less impervious to moisture?

'The child breathes air, drinks water, sees steam, hail, and snow. What are all these? the child naturally inquires, and why is the last *white*, and when melted turns into water? What are thunder and lightning, and are they of any use? The sun to him appears always round, not so the moon—why so? The principal parts of his own body, and those of other animals, with their relative functions, ought to be known; the qualities and names of the more common minerals, and the great outlines of botany, &c. Such oral training lessons ought to be commenced in their outlines in the Initiatory School, and carried forward more minutely in the juvenile and senior departments.' (pp. 185-187.)

To teachers located in the country, he offers the following suggestions and practical hints:—

'Agricultural Schools.—Although very few of you have the opportunity of actually practising farming, yet you ought to conduct *training lessons* on its various principles of chemical manure, crops, &c., and ploughing, digging, harrowing, sowing, reaping, &c., &c., which can of course be carried out more practically in country schools. We would recommend the practice of making occasional excursions into the country with your pupils, to collect specimens, thus uniting practice and theory. On the same principle, in teaching geometry, the pupils' attention ought frequently to be called to the application which may be made of the abstract truths demonstrated. Were the pupil, after demonstrating the propositions on which the measurement and calculations rest, to be required actually to measure a rectangular field, and calculate its contents—interest in the study would be greatly increased ; he would see a meaning and a use in every line he draws, and every figure he sketches.

'Were every parish or district school furnished with specimens of its peculiar plants, flowers, minerals, and living animals, which might be collected by the children of the school, not only would their minds be enlarged by *daily training lessons*, on each in succession, but the metropolitan museum of such a country might, by the peculiar specimens collected from each parish, present a complete compendium of the natural history of the whole kingdom.' (p. 341).

Stow's examples of how arithmetic and book-keeping should be taught on the training system are extremely interesting. I can afford space for the latter only.

'Book-keeping.—Pupils should be trained by *actually keeping* books in school. They might be provided with miniature sets of books, viz., journals, ledgers, cash-books, invoice-books, purchasing-ledgers, bank-books, &c., and actually required *to do the thing*, to insert the real or supposed transactions, and balance their books accordingly. Books of very small value would be sufficient for the purpose. Whilst as good figures would thus be taught as on the old plan, book-keeping would be acquired — an interest would be felt by the boys, and a bustle exhibited during the half hour of these real transactions in school resembling the aspect of a large mercantile establishment. At first, of course, simple entries would only be made of simple transactions in purchases, sales, receipts of monies, and banking arrangements; but, progressively, every variety of mercantile books would be brought into requisition, and double entry, in its most perfect form, attained.

'Boys, so trained, not simply taught, might then present their school productions as a claim to clerkships, and they would not enter counting-houses *ignoramuses*, as they now do.

'It may be stated, as an objection to the

necessity, or capability, of a teacher teaching real book-keeping in school, that every mercantile house has its own mode of keeping books. This is true; but the principle of keeping books is the same whether only three or four books are kept, or twenty, and whether they are kept by single or by double entry.' (p. 294.)

II. I now proceed to the second feature of the training system, viz., 'Picturing out,' which is distinct from pictorial illustration, or illustrating by pictures and diagrams. 'Picturing out' is effected by 'words' only, and may be described as oral illustration or 'word painting.' For example, if it were desired to picture out the meaning of the term 'evaporation,' instead of telling the children that it is the *act* or *state* of *passing off in vapour*, which might convey no better meaning to them than the word 'evaporation' by itself, it would be necessary to ask the children whether they had ever gone out to the fields or woods on a sunny day immediately after a shower, and whether they had then observed steam rising from the ground in many places. Most of them would answer 'yes,' when the teacher would remark, 'Well, then, what you see rising up is also called "vapour," and that which is taking place is called, "evaporation." A few more remarks on the subject would complete the picture. Again, if the teacher wished to picture out the meaning of 'effectual calling,' instead of explaining in the ordinary way that it means 'calling with efficiency or success,' he would say, 'Now, children, if you chanced to be amusing yourselves in the playground, and your father or mother were to come to the gate, and, wishing to speak to you, were to call aloud, and you heard the call, and ran to meet them, that would be calling with effect, or "effectual calling." The natural picture being thus conveyed to the children's minds, the spiritual picture is easily sketched—*e. g.*, the teacher might add, 'We are all by nature at a distance from God in consequence of sin, and God, in His infinite love, is constantly calling upon us through His Spirit to go to Him. When we hear, and seek to do His will, our hearts yearning after Him, we are effectually called, and become His children by grace, as well as by creation.'

Mr. Stow regarded this picturing out as one of the chief agencies in the training system. 'It is,' he says, 'a fundamental principle of the system; and whatever the school exercise may be, secular or sacred, picturing out should uniformly be adopted, both in the broad outlines and minuter points of every lesson.' (p. 190.)

'Pestalozzi was the first who introduced the systematic use of objects and prints in public education. The training system has added the systematic picturing out in words of every abstract term, figurative word, and figurative phrase, by analogy, familiar illustrations, questions and ellipses mixed, and simultaneous answers. It must be borne in mind that every word, in any language, either represents an object, or a combination of objects, and therefore may be pictured out and simplified in words representing such.' (p. 191.)

'In reading a book, or listening to a lecture or sermon, should even one figurative word or phrase be used which has not been pictured out to the mind of the auditory, that word or phrase may be a barrier to the understanding of the whole subject;* hence the slow progress of knowledge in the world, as we have already stated, and the necessity of a previous school training, and a picturing out by analogy and familiar illustrations of all figurative words and phrases used in elementary, scientific, and Scriptural education. Picturing out to the mind is still more necessary, when not merely one figura-

* True to a certain extent; but it is equally true that children pick up the meaning of a new or difficult word from its connexion with other words, if these are clear to them, in the context. See Abbott's "Teacher."

tive word is used, but when a number are presented in a single sentence. For example, Dr. Buckland, in giving "proofs of design in the effects of disturbing forces on the strata of the earth," thus expresses himself :—" *Elevations* and *subsidences, inclinations*, and *contortions, fractures* and *dislocations* are *phenomena* which, although at first sight they present only the appearance of disorder and confusion, yet, when fully understood, demonstrate the existence of order, and method, and *design*, even in the operations of the most *turbulent* among the mighty physical forces which have affected the *terraqueous* globe." We know such sentences are read in schools, without one word having been pictured out; the dictionary, with its verbal explanations, alone being accessible to the pupil; and grown-up persons peruse the same words without attaching any definite idea to them, and, finding no definitions, or rather familiar illustrations, of technical phrases in a dictionary, the sense of the author is lost to them, from the fact of the words they meet with not having been pictured out in their early education.' (p. 193.)

Picturing is best carried out, in Mr. Stow's opinion, by a skilful combination of question and answer, along with ellipses; questions alone being *dry* and setting the mind of the pupils too much on the defensive. 'Questions set the mind astir—ellipses direct what has been set a moving,' both being necessary to effect a simple, vivid, and truthful picture.

'Students, when they first enter the seminary, uniformly confine themselves to putting questions—the proper mode of putting ellipses combined with questions is a high attainment in practical training. The union affords the most pleasing, the most natural, and the most efficient of all methods of cultivating the understanding.' (p. 233.)

In picturing out, it is equally desirable to use familiar illustrations, 'such as are within the range of the experience of the children, of whatever age or condition in life. The prince, the peasant, and the factory child would generally be familiar with very different things, or, at least, would more readily apprehend the analogy of different things—and this must be left to the judgment of the trainer. As a suitable model, we have only to look into the narrative of our Saviour's life, who spoke of corn-fields, and figs, and vines, and hens, to farmers, husbandmen, and vine-dressers. Had he lived in this country, and in our day, He might have illustrated His sayings by the water-conduit, the blast-furnace, or the steam-engine.' (p. 246.)

Picturing is especially necessary in Bible-training, as every page of Scripture is full of figurative expressions. Our Saviour adopted this method of illustration in His daily teaching. 'When asked by the Pharisees, "Is it lawful to give tribute to Cæsar?" He said, "Show me a penny," &c. He did not *tell*, but *trained*. Again, when asked, "Who is my neighbour?" He pictured it out by the story of the "Good Samaritan." When John the Baptist sent his disciples to Jesus, and inquired, "Art thou he that should come, or do we look for another?" He neither answered yes nor no, but said, "Go, and shew John again those things which ye do hear and see, the blind receive their sight, and the lame walk," &c., leaving them to form the conclusion from the simple picture he had drawn.' (p. 56.)

Mr. Stow gives the following example of the principle of picturing out, taken from a Bible lesson given at the Normal School on one occasion :—

'A highly-educated M.P. was present, who expressed himself satisfied that the training system was well worthy of attention; but that he did not precisely understand the distinction between teaching and training. The master-trainer said, "Sir, you perceive that the children are now reading part of the history of the oppression of the children of Israel in Egypt, and the next part of the chapter they are about to read is regarding their using straw in the making of bricks, &c. Now, sir, I believe they do not know why straw was used, nor do they know whether the bricks in Egypt were dried in the sun, or burned as in this country." The trainer put a few questions to the children, which proved that they did not know, as he supposed. The master also said, "Were I to tell them, seeing they do not know, that would be *teaching;* but I shall not tell them, and I shall cause them to tell me the nature of the clay in Egypt, compared with that in England, and whether the bricks were burned or dried there, and that will be *training.*"

'The trainer repeated the fact that straw was used in the making of bricks in Egypt, as the children read from the Bible; but of course they were ignorant of the reason why straw was used in their manufacture. He then *brought out from them*, by analogy, the difficulty of breaking a bunch of straw, however thin—what the effect would be of layers of straw being mixed with clay, while yet in a soft state, and afterwards dried—that the straw would strengthen it, and render it more tenacious, or, at least less liable to break. He then brought out from the children that the bricks were not burned in Egypt, seeing, as they told him, that if so, the straw used would have been of no service, as in the process of burning the bricks, the straw must be reduced to ashes; that straw in this country would be of no use in the making of bricks, seeing that we burned them, and that we could not get them sufficiently dried in ordinary seasons by the sun, even in summer.

'From the nature of the climate of Egypt, with which they were acquainted, it having been brought out in some of their ordinary geography lessons, they inferred that the bricks might be dried in the sun—that the clay could not be so firm, or solid, or tenacious as ours, when they required straw to strengthen it. They therefore thought that the clay in Egypt must be more sandy than ours, seeing that our brick-makers do not require to use straw to strengthen the bricks. Thus the mode of drying bricks in Egypt, and the nature of their clay compared with ours, was determined by analogy and familiar illustrations without *telling*.' (p. 247.)

In pursuing this course of illustration, it is not necessary to explain every point in the lesson.

'Be content,' he says, 'with illustrating one distinct point during each lesson. Make use of all the knowledge the children may have previously acquired; do not take the honey, as it were, out of other flowers not analogous, and put it into the one presented, as if you had made a discovery of what really is not in the text; but take the sweets out of the one daily presented, in all their variety. Consider the effect of 300 points per annum clearly pictured out, and that number added for three, five, or seven years in succession, how luminous would the pages of Scripture appear during private reading, or while listening to a Gospel ministry!' (p. 373.)

One great advantage of the system of 'picturing out' is that it is inexhaustible. To objects, pictures, prints, and diagrams, there is obviously a limit; but to picturing out there is none, and it is also equally applicable to any subject. Thus Latin grammar might be rendered a less dry and more interesting study were the learner not permitted to use any term which had not been first pictured out to his mind; for example, such words as participle, perfect, indicative, pluperfect, subjunctive, &c.; why a noun is declined, and a verb conjugated, and the same in English grammar, objective, possessive, &c. This, I confess, would present considerable difficulty to a young teacher.

I shall conclude this subject by giving an instance, recorded by Stow, of the absurdity of using abstract terms in addressing children. 'After the public examination of a charity school in a certain manufacturing town in Scotland, a learned gentleman present was invited to put a few questions to the children. The gentleman proceeded : " Children, look at me—and answer a few questions—be very attentive—answer me this —hem! *Is it not a fact that mutation is stamped on all sublunary objects ?* " The children of course remained silent. *Mutation*, to them, was a mere sound without meaning ; *stamped* (it being a town where muslins are manufactured) only suggested to them the idea of stamping gauze, or jaconet for tambouring ; *sublunary* had never come under the category of their reading, and the term had not been analysed or explained—to them the word was therefore quite incomprehensible ; and as to *objects*, in connection with the other un-pictured-out words, they naturally thought of lame beggars who were carried from door to door on a " handbarrow," it being common to term all disabled persons *objects*—" such and such a one," they were accustomed to say, " is quite an object." ' (p. 194.) And again,—

'A reverend gentleman, examining the children of a Sabbath School, put the following question: "Children, in the work of regeneration, can you tell me whether the Spirit operates causally or instrumentally?" If these children could have answered this question, they might certainly have been transplanted, we think, to the divinity hall of a university.' (p. 195.)

III. The third characteristic of the training system is the 'sympathy of numbers,' which Mr. Stow calls the 'oil-spring' of the whole system. Every teacher of experience is aware that it is easier to teach a number of children all about the same stage of progress than to teach a few. In the one case, the potent stimulant of emulation, and of what the French call *esprit de corps* can be skilfully and successfully applied; in the other case, there is likely to be listlessness on the part of the pupils, and indifference on the part of the teacher. By all means, then, the active teacher should have a good handful of children; and fortunately, in elementary schools, there is little or no probability of any other state of matters. This being the case, I shall touch very briefly on this topic, giving my reader an opportunity of hearing Mr. Stow say a few words on the subject:—'In conducting an intellectual lesson with half a dozen children in a class of different ages like a family, the questioning must all be individual; whereas with a gallery of seventy or eighty of nearly the same age (and the nearer the better), the questioning, and development, and training may be conducted chiefly simultaneously; and thus whatever answers are brought out by the trainer, from one or more of the children, can be made the possession of all, so that every one may learn what any one knows — thus diffusing knowledge more widely, and causing the variety of natural talents and dispositions to operate favourably on all. A similar effect takes place in the moral development of dispositions and habits in the playground, some particular instances of which should be noticed by the trainer, on the return of the children to the school-gallery, and when, again, the sympathy of numbers operates favourably in applauding the good deed, or condemning the misdemeanour. There is a power, therefore, in numbers, not experienced in individual teaching or training; and the playground and the gallery conjoined, under proper management and superintendence, afford *the most perfect sympathy.*

'Whilst the pupils sympathize with each other, it is important that they sympathize also with their master. For this purpose, it is necessary that he place himself on such terms with his pupils as that they can, without fear, make him their confidant, unburden their minds, and tell him of any little mischief they may have done. Teachers and parents, desirous of gaining the confidence of their children, must in fact themselves, as it were, become children, by bending to, and occasionally engaging in, their plays and amusements. Without such condescension, a perfect knowledge of real character and dispositions cannot be obtained.' (p. 156.)

The only exception that can be taken to these observations is with respect to the number of children that can be managed in the gallery, and, indeed, the strongest objection I have heard brought against Stow's system is its too simultaneous character. In order to have them well in hand, the number, I think, should never exceed forty; * otherwise the teacher can never attain the requisite individual knowledge of the pupils and their acquirements, which his duty to them and to their parents, and the necessities of the standard examinations, require. On visiting the excellent schools recently opened by the Merchant Company in Edinburgh, with one of which—viz., the girl's school in Queen

* The practice in Norway, I believe, is to allow only twenty-five pupils to each teacher.

Street—I was much pleased; and in which 1,200 girls receive an excellent secondary and primary education combined, I was glad to find that forty is the maximum number in all the classes.

IV. The fourth feature of the book is its advocacy of the mixed system in schools, *i.e.*, that boys and girls should be taught together. At first sight, this system appears perhaps to many to be attended with considerable disadvantages, the girls being exposed by it to the natural rudeness of the boys. But after careful consideration and lengthened experience, I am decidedly of opinion that the mixed system is the best. In the practising schools of the Glasgow Church of Scotland Normal School, there are, on an average year by year, over 1,200 children in attendance, the sexes balancing each other pretty equally, and during my connexion with these schools for the past eighteen years, I have never heard nor known of any evil existing or being complained of in connexion with the system. Other training colleges afford equally good examples; the advantages of the system being quite apparent in all. Each sex seems to take from the other what it stands most in need of, the girls softening and refining the boys, while the latter sharpen and strengthen the minds and the characters of the girls; or, in the words of Mr. Stow, the 'girls morally elevate the boys, and the boys intellectually elevate the girls.'

My own experience is that boys become less rude in language and in manner, and more careful in dress and personal habits, while the minds of the girls derive equal advantages from competition with the boys. Girls, for instance, do not naturally take to arithmetic as a branch of study; but, in consequence of the stimulating presence of boys in the same class, they come to equal them, and often to excel them in calculation. Girls, too, are naturally inclined to read in too low and feeble tones, were it not that the louder and bolder style of the boys effects a cure. In teaching vocal music, again, the two sexes are almost indispensable. In this system, of course, there is a happy medium, as in everything else. While the schools, above referred to, are mixed, each sex has a playground for itself; the girls and boys of the same class sit on separate benches, and do not interchange places in the work of the class; and a mistress is associated with the master in each department. At the present time, when the attention of the country is being turned, through the operation of the Education Acts of 1870 and 1872, to the best methods of school organization, it is most important that school boards should study the question fairly, and consider whether in places where existing accommodation is deficient, they should erect large boys' schools, or girls' schools, or adopt the principle so strongly recommended by Mr. Stow. The general practice in Scotch elementary schools, from the days of Knox till now, has been that boys and girls should be taught together; and on the authority of Mr. Stow, 'the Scots are the most moral people on the face of the earth.' The model of the family circle, where brothers and sisters are brought up together; that of the social circle, where men and women mix freely in friendly intercourse, should be the basis on which the consideration of the system is made to rest. It is generally admitted that boys who have no sisters are less cultivated and refined than those who have; and why should an atmosphere, that has been proved to be so healthy at home, be considered hurtful at school? If boys and girls, young men and young women, may dance, and sing, and play, and amuse themselves together with advantage, is there any special danger to be apprehended if they should also study together? The system has been tested in America, and found to succeed admirably.

'At Oberlin College, in the State of Ohio,

where the pupils number a thousand, half of them women, the ages vary from seventeen to seven and twenty; and there the system has been in successful operation for more than five and thirty years. The testimony of the professors is unanimous, to the effect that the general tone of the students, not only as to conduct, but also as to industry, is far superior to what is usual in colleges managed on the separate principle. Cases of ungentlemanly behaviour are almost unknown.' * Equally happy results might be quoted in the case of other colleges; indeed, in the Western States the separate system has almost ceased to exist. 'The reason which led the United States into the adoption of this system was the difficulty of providing in any other way for the proper education of women. To create for them duplicate schools and colleges throughout the land with preceptors co-equal in knowledge and competency would have been financially impossible; places for joint education were therefore established, while numbers of those, originally intended for the male sex only, have one after another abandoned their exclusive traditions.' * If a corresponding abandonment were to take place in England, say in the large schools of Eton,

* Mixed Education, in "Contemporary Review," July, 1873.

Harrow, and Rugby, and the mixed system to be generally adopted, the evils deprecated by Locke and Cowper, and acknowledged by Dr. Arnold, might be in a great measure mitigated, or come to cease altogether. There is no doubt that the influence of one sex over another must take a higher rank in education than it has done, as a powerful means for moulding the human mind and character.

V. The fifth feature is the conjoint use made of the gallery and the playground for moral training. Mr. Stow was of opinion that the children should not go home at mid-day, but that having brought lunch with them, they should spend the interval in the playground, where various employments and amusing games should be provided for them. The teacher at the same time should be present in their midst, directing their amusements, and observing their actions, and in consequence gaining gradually a knowledge of the dispositions of his various pupils. The playground afforded, in Mr. Stow's opinion, an ample field for the latter object, being in fact, a world in miniature, where each little man acts his part and shews himself in his natural character. Notes having been thus taken by the teacher from day to day, the following is an example of the use to be made of them in the gallery:—'We shall suppose that in the playground one boy steals his playfellow's toy,—it may be a ball or a spinning top—the teacher sees this, or is told of it; he takes no notice of the circumstance at the moment, but on entering the school, as usual, he commences the process of examination by telling a story about a boy, who stole his neighbour's top, or something else; in a moment *the culprit's head hangs down;* it is unnecessary to mark him out,—*he is visible to all;* ninety-nine out of the hundred (if we except the injured party) sit in cool judgment upon the case, and, at the master's desire, are requested to award the punishment due to such an offence. In the meantime, he forgets not to remind the child and all present, that, though he had not observed him, God assuredly had; or rather the teacher draws out this statement from the children themselves—the *panel at the bar* remaining *perfectly quiescent.* The question may be put. *What punishment?* Some of the more furious boys, whose energies require perhaps only to be regulated in order to make them *noble* characters, call out, *Beat him, cuff him,* all the rest in the meantime keeping silence, conceiving such punishment to be rather severe. The master, however, will ask another question or two, rather than fulfil the commands of this unmerciful jury. " Is this boy in the habit of stealing your playthings?" No, sir. "None of you have seen him do such a thing till ... *now*. Then you think this is a ... *first offence?* Ought a child to be punished as severely for a *first*, as a second or third offence?" No, sir. "What then shall we do to this boy?" Instantly the girls will naturally cry out, "Forgive him, forgive him." Now, mark the natural effect upon all parties, the guilty is condemned by his fellows,—the milder feelings are brought into play, and all have been exercised in the principles of truth and justice. Without wasting words, by carrying out the probable conversation, or stating the various ramifications, which this circumstance and similar of daily occurrence among children, may present,—for not only may the playthings have been stolen, but a lie told to hide the act, and even blows given in the way of defence, all of which require distinct modes of treatment, and, if not early checked, will harden the conscience, and strengthen the evil propensities of our common nature, whatever effect the examination may have on the guilty individual, we are quite sure it will be most salutary upon all the others.' (p. 205.) Mr. Stow's opinion, on the efficiency of this superintendence at play, is very strongly expressed. 'It is as impracticable for a teacher to train morally and intellectually without a gallery, and a playground, as it would be for a mechanic to work without his tools' (p. 204). And again, 'The training system is not practised where moral superintendence of the children, by the masters, while at play, and a subsequent review of their conduct on their return to the school-gallery, forms no part of the plan pursued.' (p. 27.)

This playground superintendence, if it could be faithfully carried out, would no doubt form a valuable means, not only of moral training, but of protecting and encouraging the weaker children; but, considering the claims made upon the elementary teacher, I do not think that, with a due regard to health, he can attempt to accomplish it. If a teacher is in attendance from 8 A.M. till 12, and from 1 till 4, for the instruction of pupil teachers and children, and, in addition, corrects exercises and prepares lessons at home, it would be hard to condemn him, in a dinnerless condition, to walk sentry in the playground, even for the excellent purpose intended by the training system. An arrangement, however, might be come to whereby a second master, or sometimes a senior pupil-teacher might (by having a separate dinner hour assigned to him) overtake the work. In order to relieve the masters of the practising schools, I tried for two or three years the practice of sending the students into the playgrounds for that purpose, a week at a time; but the plan did not answer my expectations, the young men not feeling interested in the work, and, besides, the person who takes the notes of character should invariably give the moral training lesson in the gallery.

I have now gone over the main features of Stow's book; taken a run through the chief rooms of the house, as it were. There are odd corners in it, however, well worthy of inspection. For example, Mr. Stow advocates strongly the importance of physical exercises *in* and *out* of school, with a view to promote health, to perform correct habits of body, and to relieve the tedium of lessons. 'After some practice,' he says, 'a gallery of children should be able to rise up and sit down simultaneously, as perfectly as a regiment of soldiers would fire a volley, and so free from bustle in fact, that a mouse, in the act of stealing cheese, would not be disturbed.' The taking of places, and the giving of prizes, Mr. Stow views with disfavour, and he expresses himself very strongly against corporal punishment and expulsion. 'If the teacher does his duty, and uses the moral means within his reach, the use of the rod is quite unnecessary.' He is in favour of the phonic system of teaching to read, and is opposed to the employment of monitors, inquiring whether a young and inexperienced lad should take the place of a mature and cultivated teacher. He has no objection to their being made use of in such minor duties as revising the lessons in arithmetic or spelling, putting aside the pens, and other little matters that may serve to ease the labour of the master; but it cannot be expected that they should morally or intellectually train, analyse, or picture out any point or difficulty, as the master himself can do. His observations on the qualities of a good trainer are excellent—'the voice and the eye constituting,' in his opinion, 'fully one-half of his power. A trainer's manner may be said to be half his fortune.'

Stow's system was received with much favour, and its educative value has been recognised by persons of the highest position. On the authority of his biographer, I may state that the Marquis of Lansdowne, when Lord President of the Privy Council, frankly said, 'that all the improvements in education that have of late years appeared in England worth mentioning, can be easily traced to the Glasgow Normal School.'* The book is specially valuable and suggestive to Sabbath-school teachers, ministers, and home-teachers, whom the severe requirements of the Revised Code have not driven out of the pleasant God-frequented paths of moral training.

* " Memoir," p. 220.

HERBERT SPENCER.

Spencer would have the Scholastic World revise its Task—His estimate of the true 'Measure of Value' in Knowledge—Classification of the leading 'Activities' of Life—Science best fits a man for these Spheres of Activity—Science versus Language — On Intellectual Education — Old Methods of Teaching—The New should conform to Nature—Self-development should be encouraged — Education begins in the Cradle — Object Lessons — The Acquirement of Knowledge should be made Pleasurable — Moral Discipline — Natural Consequences — Practical Maxims and Rules for Moral Education.

IN Herbert Spencer we have an educationist still living, whose views are not the result of practice in the work of teaching. Such a man's thoughts and suggestions are, however, eminently noteworthy and serviceable. Standing apart from the school, he is unbiassed by the littlenesses which insensibly influence the teacher's character; and, viewing the domain of practical teaching from a distance, he is in a better positic for taking a comprehensive and perspectiv view of the teacher's sphere of action.

The education which Spencer discusses has a scope far above and beyond the elementary teacher's province; but notwithstanding this, the latter will derive much benefit from hearing what he has to say.

In perusing his Essays one is reminded of Pestalozzi, and in several respects the two men agree. If it can be said of Pestalozzi that he compelled the scholastic world to revise their task, it may be said with equal truth of Spencer, that he would compel the same course at the present time. Looking round on the domain of teaching calmly and sarcastically, he says, quietly, 'Ladies and gentlemen, the system you pursue is more suited for monks than for intelligent citizens of the nineteenth century. And not only is your system bad, but what you do teach is taught in a wrong order. Highly abstract studies, such as grammar, which should come late, are begun early. Political geography, dead and uninteresting to a child, and which should be an appendage of sociological studies, is commenced betimes, while physical geography, comprehensible and comparatively attractive to a child, is in great part passed over; you take up a child's time in teaching him dead languages, which he shall never turn to practical use, instead of teaching him the living facts of the world around him, and which have a bearing for good or for evil on his whole life. And then, pervading the whole, is the vicious system of learning by rote, by which you sacrifice the spirit to the letter; in fact, ladies and gentlemen, had there been no teaching but such as goes on in our public schools, England would now be what it was in feudal times. The vital knowledge, that by which we have grown as a nation to what we are, and which now underlies our whole existence, is a knowledge that has got itself taught in nooks and corners, while the ordained agencies for teaching have been mumbling little else but dead formulas.' *

Such a charge applies chiefly, of course, to our large public schools and universities; yet it startles the thoughtful teacher, and if he humbly sits down at the feet of this new apostle, crying, so to speak, in the wilderness, he will rise in some degree a sworn disciple, for the gospel he preaches is in the main true and convincing, as it cannot but be, since, like the teaching of Pestalozzi, it conducts one to the feet of Nature herself. The first question which you naturally put, is—'Pray, shew how my teaching is false;' and in reply the master

* " Education," pp. 25-30.

leads you into a most interesting investigation into the relative value of knowledges, which forms the subject of the first Essay in his book. The mode in which this investigation is conducted is quite after the manner of Socrates. Your inquiries are not answered at once; but he puts, as it were, two or three questions to you, and leads you by the concessions you make to answer the inquiries for yourself. 'In order to ascertain what we should teach,' he says, 'we must first of all determine what we want to be at in teaching—what our object is in teaching at all? Before there can be a rational curriculum, we must settle which things it concerns us most to know.' (p. 7.) The joint conclusion come to is, that the true 'measure of value' is the bearing which each branch of knowledge has upon some part of life—life in the highest and broadest sense; and the problem of life, as far as this world is concerned, resolves itself into the following propositions:—How to treat the body; how to treat the mind; how to manage our affairs; how to bring up a family; in what way to behave as a citizen; in what way to utilize those sources of happiness which nature supplies; how to use all our faculties to the greatest advantage of ourselves and others; how to live completely. 'To prepare us for complete living, then, is the function which education has to discharge; and the only rational mode of judging of an educational course is to judge in what degree it discharges such function,' (p. 8)—about as good a definition of education as can well be made.

Tested by this measure of value, the knowledge which has, as a rule, been laid down in every educational system, has been worthless; the knowledge which conduces to personal well-being having been postponed to that which brings applause. 'In the Greek schools, music, poetry, rhetoric, and a philosophy which, until Socrates taught, had but little bearing upon action, were the dominant subjects, while knowledge, aiding the arts of life, had a very subordinate place. And in our own universities and schools at the present moment, the like antithesis holds. What use does a boy make of his Latin and Greek in the shop or the office, in managing his estate or his family, in playing his part as a director of a bank or a railway? And in a girl's education, dancing, deportment, the piano, singing, drawing—what a large space do these occupy? And if you ask why Italian and German are learnt, you will find that under all the sham reasons given, the real reason is that a knowledge of those tongues is thought lady-like. It is not that the books written in them may be utilized, which they scarcely ever are; but that Italian and German songs may be sung, and that the extent of attainment may bring whispered admiration. The births, deaths, and marriages of kings, and other like historical trivialities, are committed to memory, not because of any direct benefits that can possibly result from knowing them; but because society considers them parts of a good education—because the absence of such knowledge may bring the contempt of others.' (pp. 2, 3.)

With a view to determine more exactly the kinds of knowledge that should be imparted, and their proper order, he classifies the leading kinds of activity, which constitute human life, into—

I. Those activities which directly minister to self-preservation.

II. Those activities which, by securing the necessaries of life, indirectly minister to self-preservation.

III. Those activities which have for their end the rearing and discipline of offspring.

IV. Those activities which are involved in the maintenance of proper social and political relations, and—

V. Those miscellaneous activities which fill up the leisure part of life, devoted to the gratification of the tastes and feelings. (p. 9.)

A few minutes' reflection will shew that these stand in something like their proper order, and the elementary teacher will find it interesting to consider how far his school-work bears on any or all of them. In Spencer's opinion that only can be called true education which prepares for these several duties, and which maintains a due proportion between the degrees of preparation in each. In respect to the first, Spencer remarks that, as it is too momentous to be left to our blundering, nature takes it into her own hands, a fact which may be traced in every instinct of the child prompting it to shrink from new or unusual sights or sounds; it is nature that trains the infant to balance its body, to control its movements so as to avoid collisions, teaches it what objects are hard, and will hurt if struck, and what things will give pain if touched, and adds to its store of knowledge from hour to hour; and, at a later stage, it is nature that trains and develops its muscles, and sharpens its perceptions by running, leaping, and jumping, and prepares it to meet those greater dangers that occasionally occur in the lives of all. All this, too, nature does in the most rigid disciplinary way, effect succeeding cause with unerring and educative yet kindly precision. All that is wanted in this fundamental education, therefore, is that there be no thwarting of nature. Stupid schoolmistresses must not be allowed to debar the girls in their charge from the spontaneous physical activities they would indulge in; and thus render them comparatively incapable of taking care of themselves in circumstances of peril. (p. 14.) In due time, however, Nature's laws of health and disease must be studied, for diseases are often contracted, our members are often injured by causes which superior knowledge would avoid. So profound is the ignorance of the laws of life that men do not even know that their sensations (when not rendered morbid by long-continued disobedience) are their natural and trustworthy guides. If fatigue of body or brain were in every case followed by desistance, if the oppression produced by a close atmosphere always led to ventilation, if there were no eating without hunger, or drinking without thirst, if, in fact, the principles of physiology were better understood and attended to, there would be fewer cases of disease and premature death. There is scarcely any one who, in the course of his life, has not brought upon himself illnesses which a little information would have saved him from. Here is a case of rheumatic fever that followed reckless exposure, there is a case of eyes spoiled for life by over-study. Hence, in Spencer's opinion, such a course of physiology as is needful for comprehending its general truths and their bearings on daily conduct is an all-essential part of a rational education.

Here I think the schoolmaster might lend a helping hand; few schools at present are without lessons in science of some kind, and I agree with Spencer in thinking that physiology is a science of primary importance. It is not necessary to go into the subject very deeply; the broad facts of the science and the rules of health being all that it is necessary to impart. The objection that is sometimes brought against it on the ground of its unsuitability for mixed classes can be easily obviated by giving separate lessons to boys and girls. Spencer expresses unmingled surprise that while parents are anxious that their sons should be well up in the superstitions of two thousand years ago, they care not that they should be taught anything about the structure and functions of their own bodies; and that men, who would blush if caught saying Iphigénia instead of Iphigenia, or would resent as an insult any imputation of ignorance respecting the fabled labours of Hercules, shew not the slightest shame in confessing that they do not know where the Eustachian tubes are, what are the actions of the spinal cord, what is the normal rate of pulsation, or how the lungs are inflated, so terribly in our education does the ornamental override the useful. (p. 17.) 'This,' says the author of "Educational Reformers," 'is begging the question,' and certainly it is to some extent; the mere facts gathered in the way of any course of study being in a measure secondary to the power of application gained in the acquisition. Spencer's opinions, it will be observed, are similar to Locke's, the latter advising us first to put the body right that it may be able to obey the behests of the mind; the former going the length of saying that the first requisite to success in life is to be a good animal. 'The best brain is of little service if there be not enough vital energy to work it.' (p. 60.)

In connection with his observations on the activities which minister to self-preservation, Spencer's Essay on Physical Education should be read. It bears chiefly on the duties of parents, but is none the less useful to teachers. The physical education of children he takes to be seriously faulty in many respects. 'It errs in deficient feeding, in deficient clothing, in deficient exercise (among girls at least),* and in excessive mental application.' (p. 188.) He is an unsparing foe to the cramming system, and wisely observes that those who, in eagerness to cultivate their pupils' minds are reckless of their bodies, do not remember that success in the world depends more on energy than on information; and that a policy, which in cramming with information undermines energy, is self-defeating. (p. 185.) Of the truth of this I have seen in student life more than one illustration; a striking case occurring to my memory at this moment, that of a young man full of promise, who used to 'say off' all his tasks, even the driest page in history, with scrupulous accuracy to the dullest detail, and who, soon after he had begun the actual work of teaching, died of congestion of the brain.

In regard to the second activity of life—that which is necessary to gain a livelihood—there is no difference of opinion as to its immense importance, and ordinary school work does in a great measure bear directly upon it; yet, while acknowledging that reading, writing, and arithmetic are taught with an intelligent appreciation of their uses, Spencer says that this is about all that is done to fit youth for the business of

* See on this subject "Nausicaa," by Rev. Charles Kingsley, in " Good Words," for January, 1874.

life. The great bulk of all the other ordinary branches taught has no bearing on the industrial activities of life, while the learning, which has, is almost entirely passed over. For, what are the great majority of men employed in? In the production, preparation, and distribution of commodities. And on what does efficiency in these industries depend? On knowledge which is in a great measure ignored in our school courses—that is, scientific knowledge. To prove this, take first mathematics. Is not some acquaintance with this science indispensable in all the higher arts of construction? The village carpenter, equally with the builder of a Britannia bridge, makes hourly reference to its principles. The surveyor, the architect, the builder, the mason, and the various artisans engaged in building a house are all guided by mathematical truths. The same remark holds for railway making, for the construction of docks and harbours, and for the sinking of mines. Out of geometry, as applied to astronomy, has grown the art of navigation, which has so enormously increased our foreign commerce. Then there is the application of mechanics on which the success of modern manufactures depends. To machinery we are indebted for almost all our comforts and luxuries. Trace the history of the breakfast roll, and think of the soil, the seed, the crop, all wrought by machinery; and the flour made into bread and biscuits by the same agency. Take the house in which you live, the clothing you wear, the book you read, are they not all products of machinery? Pass next to physics. Joined with mathematics it has given us the steam-engine, which does the work of millions of labourers; the thermometer, the microscope, the safety lamp, the mariner's compass, the telegraph. Still more numerous are our obligations to chemistry; to biology, the science of life, which underlies the operations of farming and the regulation of diet for man and brute, and to which the superiority of English to Continental farming is mainly due. Lastly, there is the science of sociology, or science of society, the students of which are men who daily look at the state of the money market, and whose mercantile operations are decided by the probable crops of corn, cotton, sugar, &c., the chances of war, the law of supply and demand, their success being dependent in every instance on the correctness of their judgment. In fact, to every one engaged in the business of life, a knowledge of science in some of its departments is of fundamental importance. And on this knowledge depends in a great degree his chance of gaining a good livelihood—and if this has been true in the past, it will be more so in the future; yet, strange to say, this knowledge is that which is almost entirely left out in our school-courses. Teach science, therefore, is the moral pointed by Mr. Spencer. But should we teach science to everybody? This is clearly impossible; and, in many instances, as Mr. Quick observes, the knowledge of the science which underlies an operation confers no practical utility whatever. 'No one sees the better for understanding the structure of the eye, and the undulatory theory of light. In swimming or rowing, a senior wrangler has no advantage over a man who is entirely ignorant about the laws of fluid pressure.'* And in many instances, as Spencer acknowledges, it is cheaper for business men to call in the aid of a man of science; the brewer, if his business is extensive, finds it pay to keep a chemist on the premises; and the landowner, who would sink a coal-mine or open up the hillside to find valuable ore, will find it profitable to call in the professional geologist or mining engineer. Spencer's remarks are true, however, to the extent that a man should by all means make it a point to study the science of his particular trade, occupation,

* "Educational Reformers," p. 236.

or profession—and teachers, as much as other men, need this advice.

In the third class of activities, viz., those which have for their end the rearing and discipline of offspring, the school-teacher has no direct interest. But parents, and especially mothers, should, in Spencer's opinion, study more or less the principles which guide school teachers in their methods of discipline. Spencer is severe on the nursery legislation of the young mother who, 'but a few years ago, was at school, where her memory was crammed with words, and names, and dates, and her reflective faculties scarcely in the slightest degree exercised—where not one idea was given her respecting the methods of dealing with the opening minds of children, and where her discipline did not in the least fit her for thinking out methods of her own. She knows nothing about the nature of the emotions, their order of evolution, their functions, or where use ends and abuse begins. This and that kind of action, which are quite normal and beneficial, she perpetually thwarts, and so diminishes the child's happiness and profit, injures its temper and her own, and produces estrangement; other actions, which she thinks it desirable to encourage, she gets performed by threats and bribes, or by exciting a desire for applause, considering little what the inward motive may be, so long as the outward conduct conforms; and thus cultivating hypocrisy, and fear, and selfishness, in place of good feeling. While insisting on truthfulness she constantly sets an example of untruth by threatening penalties which she does not inflict. While inculcating self-control, she hourly visits on her little ones angry scoldings for acts undeserving of them. She has not the remotest idea that in the nursery, as in the world, that alone is the truly salutary discipline which visits on all conduct, good or bad, the natural consequences — the consequences, pleasurable or painful, which in the nature of things such conduct tends to bring.' (pp. 27, 28.) And then the culture of her children's minds—is not this mismanaged in a similar manner? Ignorant of psychology, she thrusts a primer into the hands of her little one, instead of training it to observe the objects and processes of the household, the streets, and the fields—till it has acquired a tolerably exhaustive knowledge of which, no child should be introduced to books.'

The spirit of this protest applies likewise to untrained and unthinking teachers, who display in their modes of teaching and discipline much of the waywardness and ignorance ascribed to inexperienced parents. Spencer does not state at what stage book-learning should come in; but I am myself of opinion that if Locke's plan of 'playing' the child into learning is adopted, the primer may go on, *pari passu*, with the training of the observing powers. Books and birds, and flowers, animals and stories about them, trees and illustrative letterpress, would thus go hand in hand, each throwing light on, and adding greater interest to the other.

From the parental functions, Spencer passes to the political, and inquires what our school courses do to fit a man for his duties as a citizen. Positively nothing, he finds; for the only branch bearing on the subject is history, and what form does it commonly take? A biography of kings, and an account of battles and their causes, facts amusing and interesting enough, but of no use in enabling a man to vote judiciously at the next election. Thereupon he goes into a disquisition on what constitutes history,, properly so-called. I. Let us have an account of the government of a country, with as much information as possible about its structure, principles, methods, prejudices, corruptions, &c. II. A parallel description of its ecclesiastical government, its ceremonials, creeds, and religious ideas. III. The control exercised by class over class, as displayed in social observances, in titles, salutations, and forms of address. IV. The customs which regulated popular life indoors and out of doors, including the relations of the sexes, and the relations between parents and children. V. The prevailing superstitions. VI. The leading industries of the people, how trades were regulated, and what was the connection between employer and employed, what were the agencies for distributing commodities, what were the means of communication, what the circulating medium. VII. The intellectual condition of the nation should also be depicted, the arts and sciences illustrated, architecture, sculpture, painting, dress, music, poetry, and fiction. VIII. A sketch of the daily lives of the people, their food, homes, and amusements. IX, and last, The moral condition of the people should be carefully exhibited, as indicated in their laws, habits, proverbs, and deeds. (p. 35.)

In fact, such a mass of information as one finds in Knight's "Pictorial History of England," of seven or eight volumes, thick octavo. This, alone, is the kind of information which can be of service to the citizen in regulating his political life, and which Spencer elevates into a science, calling it "Descriptive Sociology." This is the latest of the sciences, however, and is not meant for children. If history be taught to children, it should not be history of the dry and bald type usually presented. Bare outlines, which have little or no educative value, are given first, instead of interesting stories. Dr. Arnold's plan of a child's first history book, a picture of the memorable deeds which would best appeal to the child's imagination, arranged in order of time, but with no other connection, would be infinitely preferable. Miss Yonge's "Golden Deeds" is such a book, or some book in the style of Macaulay's "Essays," suited to the capacity of children. Biographies of great men should precede any history, and as a model for biographies, we may take "Plutarch's Lives."*

And now we come to the last activity of human life, that which busies itself with the enjoyments of nature, of literature, and of the fine arts. 'Without painting, sculpture, music, poetry, and the emotions produced by natural beauty of every kind, life would lose half its charm.' (p. 37.) But as these occupy the leisure part of life, so should they occupy the leisure part

* "Thoughts and Suggestions in Educational Reformers."

of education. (p. 39.) What knowledge best fits a man for this sphere of activity? The answer is still the same—science—without which there can be neither perfect production, nor full appreciation. He that would enjoy the creations of the sculptor must, like the artist himself, be acquainted with the structure of the human frame. From ignorance of science, Mr. John Lewis, careful painter as he is, casts the shadow of a lattice-window in sharply defined lines upon an opposite wall. It is want of a knowledge of musical science that tolerates the swarms of worthless ballads that infest our drawing-rooms, which err against science by setting to music ideas that are not emotional enough to prompt musical expression. In poetry the same thing holds good; for, though the poet is born, not made, it is only when genius is married to science that the highest results can be produced. In fact, science is in itself poetic, and opens up realms of poetry where, to the unscientific, all is a blank. In proof read Hugh Miller's works on geology, or Mr. Lewes's " Sea-side Studies." What additional interest does science give in looking at nature; a drop of water, a snow flake, a rounded boulder marked with parallel scratches, plants in the hedge-row, insects in a garden, birds in the fields and woods, fossils in the neglected quarry; for the proper study and enjoyment of all these, scientific culture is the proper preparation.

In discussing the relative value of knowledges, Spencer is fully alive to the fact that knowledge has two values, value as knowledge *per se*, and value as discipline, or, in other words, a use for guiding conduct, and a use as mental exercise. So, after ascertaining the chief kinds of knowledge useful for purposes of guidance, he briefly considers what kinds are best for discipline; and the result he arrives at is that what is best for the one end is best for the other. 'It would be utterly contrary to the beautiful economy of nature,' he says, 'if one kind of culture were needed for the gaining of information, and another kind were needed as a mental gymnastic.' (p. 46.)

The result of all inquiry on this subject leads to the conclusion that the highest power of a faculty results from the discharge of those duties which the conditions of life require it to discharge; and, *à priori*, the same law holds throughout education. The education of most value for guidance must at the same time be the education of most value for discipline. (p. 47.) In evidence, he discusses the rival claims of classics and science as branches of learning. The memory is well cultivated and strengthened by the study of languages, say the classicists. The truth is, replies Spencer, that the sciences afford far wider fields for the exercise of memory. Is it a slight task to remember everything about our solar system, to remember the number of compound substances to which chemistry daily adds, to remember the enormous mass of phenomena presented by the earth's crust and by the fossils it contains, to remember the quantity of detail involved in human anatomy, the number of plants distinguished by botanists, and the varied forms of animal life estimated by zoologists? Surely, then, science, cultivated even to a very moderate extent, affords adequate exercise for memory. To say the least, it involves quite as good a discipline for this faculty as language does. And mark, further, that while for the training of mere memory, science is as good as, if not better than language, it has an immense superiority in the kind of memory it trains; in short, while language trains the memory, science exercises both memory and understanding. But Spencer seems to omit a circumstance which has a very important bearing on this discussion—viz., Would these sciences he recommends for study be understandable by children?* The upshot would be that only the *results* of the various sciences would

* "Educational Reformers," p. 233.

be attempted; and the schoolboy would be called upon to get up lists of plants and of chemicals in much the same way as he gets up lists of the Saxon kings, or of irregular verbs.

It is true that, if the elements of any single science, such as physiology or botany, were taught in a scientific way, the memory equally with the understanding would receive healthful exercise, but to substitute a course of sciences for all the linguistic learning now in practice would prove very unsuitable for youthful training. A good curriculum should have a sprinkling of both languages and science. To judge between the two, science *versus* language, as a means of discipline, the teacher should try with his own family the result of instruction in any given science, such as botany, during a summer vacation, and see whether or not the study results in a cultivation of the judgment and of the memory. I have known the observing powers of a child to be beneficially exercised in this way; but it was owing to the companionship in walks of father and son, and a constant tuition, which could not be undertaken by the school teacher.

Besides memory, says Spencer, science cultivates the judgment, an advantage not possessed by languages. On this point I cannot agree with him, as I have had personal experience to the contrary; and I know of no better field for the exercise of judgment than the critical reading of classic authors. Thirdly, he thinks that science is best for moral discipline. The learning of languages, he says, leads to dogmatic teaching, and to unquestioning submission to authority. Such and such are the meanings of the words, says the teacher or the dictionary. Quite opposite is the mental tone acquired in the cultivation of science, which makes constant appeal to individual reason, and encourages every one to test its facts. Science asks a man to believe nothing without seeing it to be true. Granted; but is it not also true that the intelligent teaching of languages proceeds on no such dogmatic ground as that which is here assumed. Lastly, says Spencer, the discipline of science is superior to that of languages, because of the religious culture that it gives, religious in the widest and highest sense. Professor Huxley echoes the sentiment when he says, " True science and true religion are twin sisters, and the separation of either from the other is sure to prove the death of both." In this sentiment, Spencer is, I think, fairly in the clouds; for, in my experience, I have not found men of science to be more religious—that is, more honourable, more honest, more truthful, more self-sacrificing—than their neighbours; and I do not see why a man who gloats over the anatomy of a chimpanzee, becomes pale and emaciated over the crucible, or spends anxious hours in calculating the wave-length of light, should necessarily, and more than the student of languages, have his thoughts turned from nature to nature's God. I have spent weeks and months in the absorbing study of botany, and under the most favourable circumstances for the creation of the religious feeling, and I cannot say that my frame of mind was more religious than when I have been engaged with other pursuits. Religious life is a thing altogether different and independent of either classics or science, and may be enjoyed to the full by a man who is ignorant of both. As regards mental discipline, the claims of languages and science are pretty equally potent, and if we limit the rivalry to *modern* languages and science, they are much on an equality as regards usefulness. And an advantage I have to claim for languages, which Spencer entirely ignores, is the command of words, and the training in composition which the study gives, while the study of science may leave a man as illiterate and powerless in the use of words as before.

This advantage, most students of science will confess, is really the conclusion which we must arrive at if experience is to be our guide.

Thus to the question, what knowledge is of most worth, the uniform reply is science. This is the verdict on all the counts. For direct self-preservation, or the maintenance of life and health, the all-important knowledge is science. For that indirect self-preservation which we call gaining a livelihood, the knowledge of greatest value is science. For the due discharge of parental functions, the proper guidance is to be found in science. For that interpretation of national life, past and present, without which the citizen cannot rightly regulate his conduct, the indispensable key is science. Alike for the most perfect production, and highest enjoyment of art in all its forms, the needful preparation is still science. And for purposes of discipline, intellectual, moral, and religious, the most efficient study is once more, science. And yet, adds the champion of science, this study, immensely transcending all others in importance, is that which in an age of boasted education receives the least attention. Science is the Cinderella in the family of knowledge, to whom has been committed all the work, and to whose skill, intelligence, and devotion all conveniences and gratifications have been due, and who has been kept in the background for centuries that her haughty sisters might flaunt their fripperies in the eyes of the world. The day is at hand, however, when the positions will be changed, and science will reign supreme, highest alike in worth and beauty. (p. 55.)

On intellectual education, which comes more directly within the sphere of the schoolmaster's duty, Spencer's book is very suggestive. His notion of what a teacher should be is very high. 'The mistress of a dame's school,' he says, 'can hear spelling lessons, and any hedge schoolmaster can drill boys in the multiplication table; but to teach spelling rightly by using the powers of the letters instead of their names, or to instruct in numerical combinations by experimental synthesis, a modicum of understanding is needful; and to pursue a like rational course through the entire range of studies asks an amount of judgment, of invention, of intellectual sympathy, of analytical faculty, which we shall never see applied to it while the tutorial office is held in such small esteem. True education is practicable only by a true philosopher. (p. 70.)

He rejoices that several old methods of teaching have been of late abandoned, among others learning by rote, about which Montaigne so pithily remarked, '*Savoir par cœur n'est pas savoir*,' and teaching by rules, giving the net product of inquiry without the inquiry that leads to it, an inefficient and enervating, easy-come, easy-go process; the new and more natural method being particulars first, and then the generalization; hence that intensely stupid custom, the teaching grammar to children, should be abandoned, grammar being, as M. Marcel puts it, not the stepping-stone, but the finishing instrument; and, as Mr. Wyse argues, 'Grammar is the science, the philosophy of language; and in following the process of nature, neither individuals nor nations ever arrive at the science *first*.' (p. 62.) He hails at the same time the advent of new practices, the most important of which is the systematic culture of the powers of observation, on the acuteness of which success in life so much depends. Artists, naturalists, and men of science all alike depend on their observing powers; the physician as much as the engineer; and who is the philosopher but one who *observes* relationships of things which others had overlooked; the poet, but one who *sees* the fine facts in nature, which all recognise when pointed out, but did not before remark. (p. 63.) And what is the common characteristic of the changes that have been made, and are now being made in teaching? Is it not an increasing conformity to the methods of nature? The relinquishment of early forcing, against which nature rebels, and the leaving of the first years for exercise of the limbs and senses shew this; the superseding of rote lessons by lessons orally and experimentally given like those of the field and play-ground shews this; the system of object lessons shews this; teaching from the concrete, the disuse of teaching by rules, and the tendency to make learning attractive, all point in the same direction. (p. 66.) In fact, we are on the high way towards the doctrine enunciated by Pestalozzi, that, alike in its order and in its methods, education must conform to the natural process of mental evolution—that there is a certain sequence in which the faculties spontaneously develop, and a certain kind of knowledge which each requires during its development, and that it is for us to ascertain this sequence and supply this knowledge. All the improvements above alluded to are partial applications of this general principle. A nebulous perception of it now prevails among teachers; and it is daily more insisted on in educational works. 'The method of nature is the archetype of all methods,' says M. Marcel. 'The vital principle in the pursuit is to enable the pupil rightly to instruct himself,' writes Mr. Wyse. (p. 66.) Pestalozzi hit the idea, but failed to work it out, and his idea remains to be realised, and it may be done, in a measure at least, by the aid of the following principles, which should guide the educator in his work. (p. 73.)

I. We should proceed from the simple to the complex, both in our choice of subjects, and in the way in which each subject is taught. We should begin with but few subjects at once, and as new faculties of the mind under training come into play, we should successively add to these, until we finally carry on all subjects abreast.

II. The development of the mind is an advance from the indefinite to the definite. First principles and thoughts are extremely vague, hence it is impossible to put precise ideas into the undeveloped mind. Some teachers suppose that when the verbal forms in which such ideas are wrapped up have been learnt, the ideas themselves have been acquired. Cross-examination proves the contrary, and it turns out either that the words have been committed to memory, with little or no thought about their meaning, or else that the perception of their meaning, which has been gained, is a very cloudy one. Be content then to set out with crude notions, trusting to time and experience to make them perfect, and the scientific formulæ should be given only when the conceptions are perfected. I confess that I agree with the author of "Educational Reformers," in not feeling very certain of the truth of this principle, or of its application if true. It is right to remember that a child's intellectual conceptions are at first vague; but this is rather a fact than a principle.

III. We should proceed from the concrete to the abstract, a principle identical in some respects with that first stated, though in others essentially different. In conformity with this principle, Pestalozzi made the actual counting of things precede the teaching of abstract rules in arithmetic. The use of the ball-frame further exemplifies it, as also does Professor De Morgan's mode of explaining the decimal notation. Marcel, repudiating the old system of tables, teaches weights and measures by referring to the actual foot and yard, pound and ounce, gallon and quart, and lets the discovery of their relationships be experimental. The use of geographical models, and models of the regular bodies, as introductory to geography and geometry respectively, is on the same principle. In this way the child's mind acquires knowledge as all mankind have learnt it. The truths of number, of form, of relationship in position, were all originally drawn from objects, and to present these truths to the child in the concrete is to let him learn them as the race learnt them. By and bye, perhaps, it will come to be seen that he can learn them in no other way, for if he is made to repeat them as abstractions, these can have no meaning for him until he finds that they are simply statements of what he intuitively discerns. (p. 64.)

IV. The education of the child must accord both in mode and arrangement with the education of mankind, considered historically; in other words, the genesis of knowledge in the individual must follow the same course as the genesis of knowledge in the race. If there be an order in which the human race has mastered its various kinds of knowledge, there will arise in every child an aptitude to acquire these kinds of knowledge in the same order. Hence education should be a repetition of civilization in little—and in deciding upon the right method of education, an inquiry into the method of civilization will help us. This thesis is of course quite beyond the sphere of the elementary teacher's duties; but two very useful conclusions result from such an inquiry.

V. One of them is, that in teaching we should proceed from the empirical to the rational, or experiment first and generalization after. In the history of human progress art has preceded science, practice and experience lead to organized knowledge or science. Every study, therefore, should have a purely experimental introduction, and only after an ample fund of observations have been accumulated should reasoning begin. As illustrative applications of this rule, we may instance the modern course of teaching language before grammar, not after it, or the ordinary custom of prefacing perspective by practical drawing. As an example of a first lesson in empirical perspective, he gives the following :—

'A plate of glass so framed as to stand vertically on the table being placed before the pupil, and a book or like simple object laid on the other side of it, the pupil is requested, while keeping the eye in one position, to make ink dots on the glass, so that they may coincide with, or hide the corners of this object. He is next told to join these dots by lines; on doing which he perceives that the lines he makes hide, or coincide with the outlines of the object. And then by putting a sheet of paper on the other side of the glass, it is made manifest to him that the lines he has thus drawn represent the object as he saw it." (p. 92.)

A series of such simple and attractive exercises will soon familiarise the pupil with the principles of the art, and give him a facility in the practice of it. First lessons in geometry should be given on a similar plan, and Mr. Wyse's method is quoted in illustration, the child to begin with a cube, which at once exhibits points, straight lines, parallel lines, angles, parallelograms, &c. From this he advances to a globe, which furnishes him with elementary notions of the circle, and of curves generally. When he is familiar with solids, he may substitute planes by an easy transition. Thus the cube can be cut into thin divisions and placed on paper, and he will then see as many plane rectangles as he has divisions; so with all the others. Globes may be treated in the same manner, and the pupil will thus perceive how surfaces really are generated, and be enabled to abstract them with facility in every solid. He has thus acquired the alphabet and reading of geometry, and he next proceeds to write it, which is most easily done by placing the planes on a piece of paper, and passing the pencil round them; and when this has been done frequently, the plane may be put at a little distance, and the child required to copy it, and so on. A stock of geometrical conceptions having been obtained, in some such manner as this, the child may be called upon to test the correctness of figures drawn by eye, and subsequently he should be required to make figures out of card-board, his efforts in which will go far to qualify him for beginning the study of rational geometry. A branch of knowledge which, as commonly taught, is dry and even repulsive, may thus, by following the method of nature, be made extremely interesting and beneficial. (p. 96.) The pupil thus trained will come to regard the demonstrations of Euclid as the missing supplements to his familiar problems. His well-disciplined faculties will enable him easily to master its successive propositions, and to appreciate their value; and he will have the occasional gratification of finding some of his own methods proved to be true. It only remains to add that his mind will presently arrive at a fit condition for that most valuable of all exercises for the reflective faculties—the making of original demonstrations. (p. 98.)

VI. In education, self-development should be encouraged to the uttermost; a second corollary from the principle, fourth in order. Children should be led to make their own investigations, and to draw their own inferences. They should be told as little as possible, and induced to discover as much as possible. Humanity has progressed solely by self-instruction, and in order to achieve the best results each mind must progress after the same fashion. 'Those who have been brought up under the ordinary school drill, and have carried away with them the idea that education is practicable only in that style, will think it hopeless to make children their own teachers. If, however, they will consider that the all-important knowledge of surrounding objects, which a child gets in its early years, is got without help—if they will remember that the child is self-taught in the use of its mother tongue—if they will estimate the amount of that experience of life, that out-of-school wisdom, which every boy gathers for himself—if they will think how many minds have struggled up unaided, not only through the mysteries of our irrationally-planned curriculum, but through hosts of other obstacles besides : they will find it a not unreasonable conclusion that, if the subjects be put before him in right order and right form, any pupil of ordinary capacity will surmount his successive difficulties with but little assistance. Who indeed can watch the ceaseless observation and inquiry and inference going on in a child's mind, or listen to its acute remarks on matters within the range of its faculties, without perceiving that these powers it manifests, if brought to bear systematically upon studies within the same range, would readily master them without help? This need for perpetual telling results from our stupidity, not from the child's. We drag it away from the facts in which it is interested, and which it is actively assimilating of itself. We put before it facts far too complex for it to understand, and therefore distasteful to it. Finding that it will not voluntarily acquire these facts, we thrust them into its mind by force of threats and punishment. By thus denying the knowledge it craves, and cramming it with knowledge it cannot digest, we produce a morbid state of its faculties; and a consequent disgust for knowledge in general. And when, as a result partly of the stolid indolence we have brought on, and partly of still continued unfitness in its studies, the child can understand nothing without explanation, and becomes a mere passive recipient of our instruction, we infer that education must necessarily be carried on thus. Having by our method induced helplessness, we make the helplessness a reason for our method. Clearly, then, the experience of pedagogues cannot rationally be quoted against the system we are advocating.

And whoever sees this will see that we may safely follow the discipline of nature throughout —may by a skilful ministration make the mind as self-developing in its later stages as it is in its earlier ones; and that only by doing this can we produce the highest power and activity.' (pp. 77-79.) This self-instruction begins, as we all know, in the cradle. The wide-eyed gaze of the infant at surrounding objects, those fingerings and suckings of everything it can lay hold of, these open-mouthed listenings to every sound, are first steps in the series which ends in the discovery of unseen planets, the invention of calculating engines, the production of great paintings, or the composition of symphonies and operas. (p. 80.) Materials on which the faculties may exercise themselves should therefore be presented in due variety; we should provide for the infant a sufficiency of objects presenting different degrees and kinds of resistance, a sufficiency of objects reflecting different amounts and qualities of light; and a sufficiency of sounds contrasted in their loudness, their pitch and their *timbre*, the earliest impressions which the mind can assimilate being the sensations produced by resistance, light, and sound. The ordinary practices of the nursery fulfil these early requirements of education to a considerable degree; but much more might be done. Object lessons should be given at a later stage, and here we must be careful not to *tell* the child the facts to be observed, but, on the contrary, we must listen to all the child has to tell us about each object; we must induce it to say everything it can think of about such objects, and occasionally draw its attention to facts it has not observed, with the view of leading it to notice them itself, wherever they recur. Further, 'object lessons should be extended to a range of things far wider, and continued to a period far later than now. They should not be limited to the contents of the house, but should include those of the fields and the hedges, the quarry, and the sea-shore. They should not cease with early childhood; but should be so kept up during youth, as insensibly to merge into the investigations of the naturalist and the man of science. Here again we have but to follow nature's leadings. Where can be seen an intenser delight than that of children picking up new flowers and watching new insects, or hoarding pebbles and shells? Every botanist who has had children with him in the woods and lanes must have noticed how eagerly they joined in his pursuits, how keenly they searched out plants for him, how intently they watched while he examined them, how they overwhelmed him with questions. The consistent follower of Bacon,—the 'servant and interpreter of nature,'—will see that we ought to adopt the mode of culture thus indicated. Having become familiar with the simpler properties of inorganic objects, the child should by the same process be led on to an exhaustive examination of the things it picks up in its daily walks, the less complex facts they present being alone noticed at first; in plants—the colours, numbers, and forms of the petals, and shapes of the stalks and leaves; in insects—the numbers of the wings, legs, and antennæ, and their colours. As these become fully appreciated and invariably observed, further facts may be successively introduced—the system pursued throughout being that of making it the child's ambition to say respecting everything it finds all that can be said. Then, when a fit age has been reached, the means of preserving plants and insects should be supplied—an admirable introduction to the study of botany and physiology.' (pp. 85, 87.)

Again, the child's earliest attempts to draw should by all means be encouraged, and here colouring should precede everything else. A box of paints and a brush, these are the treasures, and the greater delight in colour, which is not only conspicuous in children, but persists in most persons throughout life, should be continuously employed as the natural stimulus to the mastery of the comparatively difficult and unattractive form. If, before formal lessons in drawing are at all possible, we can, by furnishing cheap woodcuts to be painted, and simple outline maps to be tinted, pleasurably draw out the faculty of colour, and incidentally produce some familiarity with the outlines of things and countries, and some ability to move the brush steadily, it must happen that when the age for lessons in drawing is reached, there will exist a facility, that would else have been absent. Time will have been gained, and trouble both to teacher and pupil saved. (p. 90.)

This method of self-evolution possesses the great advantage of creating a vividness and permanency of impression which the usual methods can never produce. Any piece of knowledge which the pupil has himself acquired—any problem which he has himself solved, becomes, by virtue of the conquest, much more thoroughly his own than it could else be, or as M. Marcel expresses it, 'What the learner discovers by mental exertion is better known than what is told him.' This self-culture is of course inculcated by various other educationists, Pestalozzi, Wilderspin, and Stow.

VII. Finally, we should take care to make the acquirement of knowledge pleasurable, a principle strongly inculcated by Locke, and that is being acted on more and more. Asceticism is disappearing out of education, as out of life; lessons cease before the child evinces symptoms of weariness; there are short breaks during school hours, excursions into the country, amusing. lectures, choral songs, and other traits which denote the change that has come over the spirit of school legislation. Methods that are found to be productive of interest and delight are proved by experience to be the right methods. A pleasurable state of feeling is far more favourable to intellectual action than a state of indifference or disgust, a truth very beautifully expressed by Locke. Grave moral consequences also depend upon the habitual pleasure or pain which daily lessons produce. No one can compare the faces and manners of two boys—the one made happy by mastering interesting subjects, and the other made miserable by disgust with his studies, by consequent inability, by cold looks, by threats, by punishment—without seeing that the disposition of the one is being benefited, and that of the other injured. Both temper and health are favourably affected in the one case, while in the other there is danger of constitutional depression. There is yet another result of no small moment. The relationship between teachers and pupils is rendered friendly and influential or antagonistic and powerless, according as the system of culture produces happiness or misery. Human beings are at the mercy of their associated ideas; and a daily minister of pain cannot fail to be regarded with secret dislike, while one who encourages them to effort, and satisfies them with success cannot but be liked. (pp. 102, 103.)

This completes the list of those excellent principles, to which Spencer might have added an equally excellent one, 'from the known to the unknown,' on which every teacher of skill and experience acts every day; *e.g.*, in the teaching of geography, he begins with the noteworthy land-marks of the parish in which the school is situated, river, hills, plain, valley, and passing to the points of the compass, and to the remainder of the county (which is illustrated by a black-board drawing, or a local map), he proceeds to the whole country, and to the other countries adjacent, leaving the more distant and less known to the last. 'A marvellous instance of the neglect of this principle is found in the practice of teaching Latin grammar before English grammar. As Professor Seeley has well pointed out, children bring with them to school the knowledge of language in its concrete form. They may soon be taught to observe the language they already know, and to find, almost for themselves, some of the main divisions of words in it. But instead of availing himself of the child's previous knowledge, the schoolmaster takes a new and difficult language, differing as much as possible from English, a new and difficult science, that of grammar, conveyed, too, in a new and difficult terminology, and all this he tries to teach at the same time. The consequence is that the science is destroyed, the terminology is either misunderstood, or, more probably, associated with no ideas, and even the language for which every sacrifice is made is found in nine cases out of ten, never to be acquired at all.' *

By adhering to the foregoing principles, a taste for continuing the acquisition of knowledge in after-life will be acquired, and Spencer very truthfully adds, 'the men to whom in boyhood information came in dreary tasks, along with threats of punishment, and who were never led into habits of independent inquiry, are unlikely to be students in after

* " Educational Reformers," p. 251.

years, while those to whom it came in the natural forms, at the proper times, and who remember its facts as not only interesting in themselves, but as the occasions of a long series of gratifying successes, are likely to continue through life the self-instruction commenced in youth.' (p. 104.)

On the subject of *Moral Discipline*, Spencer has written a beautiful chapter, which every teacher and parent should read. The moral management of children is, in his opinion, lamentably low. As a general rule, the treatment to which they are subjected, is that which the impulse of the moment prompts; or if certain methods and doctrines do exist, they are those suggested by the remembrance of childhood, or those adopted from nurses and servants—methods devised not by the enlightenment, but by the ignorance of the time. 'What kind of moral discipline is to be expected from a mother, who, time after time, angrily shakes her infant, because it will not suck, which we once saw a mother do? How much sense of justice is likely to be instilled by a father who, on having his attention drawn by a scream to the fact that his child's finger is jammed between the window-sash and the sill, begins to beat the child instead of releasing it? How very different from this fitful discipline is that suggested by nature. When a child falls, or runs its head against the table, it suffers a pain, the remembrance of which tends to make it more careful; and by repetition of such experiences it is essentially disciplined into proper guidance of its movements. If it lays hold of the fire-bars, thrusts its hand into a candle-flame, or spills boiling-water on any part of its skin, the resulting burn or scald is a lesson not easily forgotten.* The impression produced has passed into a proverb, "the burnt child dreads the fire." And it should be further borne in mind, that these consequences are proportionate to the transgressions. A slight accident brings a slight pain, a more serious one a severer pain. No urchin who stumbles on the door-step suffers in excess of the amount necessary; but from his daily experience he is left to learn the greater or less penalties of greater or less errors, and to behave accordingly. And mark, those natural reactions which follow the child's wrong actions are constant, direct, unhesitating, and not to be escaped. No threats, but a silent rigorous performance. If a child runs a pin into its

* Miss Edgeworth, in "Practical Education," makes use of the same illustration.

fingers, pain follows. If it does it again, there is again the same result. In all its dealings with inorganic nature, it finds this unswerving persistence which listens to no excuse, and from which there is no appeal; and very soon recognising this stern though beneficent discipline, it becomes extremely careful not to transgress.' (p. 115.)

These truths appear more significant, when we reflect that they hold as well in manhood as in childhood. If a youth enters on life, and evinces idleness or carelessness in the duties of his situation, he is dismissed at once, and left to suffer the natural consequences of his misdoing. The unpunctual man, ever missing the appointments of business and pleasure, feels the losses and inconveniences resulting from his conduct. The train is gone, the steamboat is just leaving its moorings, or the best things in the market are sold, or all the good seats in the concert room are filled. (p. 120.) The tradesman who charges too high a rate of profit loses his customers, and so is checked in his greediness. Diminishing practice teaches the inattentive doctor to bestow more trouble on his patients, and so, throughout the life of every citizen, cause and effect succeed each other with unerring precision and regularity.

These facts suggest the true theory and practice of moral education. Parents, as 'ministers and interpreters of nature,' must see that their children habitually experience the true consequences of their conduct—neither warding them off nor intensifying them, nor putting artificial consequences in place of them. To take one or two illustrations. When a child leaves its box of toys scattered on the floor, the normal course is to make the child itself collect them. The labour of putting things in order is the true consequence of having put them in disorder. Every trader in his office, every wife in her household, has daily experience of this fact; and if education be a preparation for the business of life, then every child should have from the beginning experience of the fact. If the child refuse or neglect to pick up and put away the things, and has thereby entailed the trouble of doing this on some one else, it should, when next it wants them, be denied the pleasure of working with its toys at all, a little gentle reasoning being applied to it at the same moment. This is obviously a natural consequence, not dependent on natural caprice. Take another case. A child is never ready in time for its daily walk, never thinking of putting on its things till the others are at the door; the scolding or cuffing invariably given does not cure the evil, and nothing will but the natural penalty that should follow the unpunctuality. If Jane is not ready at the appointed time, the natural result is that of being left behind, and losing her walk. After she had once or twice remained at home, while the rest were enjoying themselves in the fields, amendment would in all probability take place. At any rate, the measure would be more effective than that perpetual scolding which ends only in producing callousness. Again, when children, through carelessness, break or lose the things given to them, the natural penalty is the loss of the article, or the cost of replacing it. This does not refer to that early period at which toys are pulled to pieces in the process of learning their physical properties, and at which the results of carelessness are not understood, but to a later period when the meaning and advantages of property are perceived. When a boy, old enough to possess a pen-knife, uses it so roughly as to snap the blade, or leaves it in the grass by some hedge-side, where he was cutting a stick, a thoughtless parent or some indulgent relation will commonly buy him another at once, not seeing that, by doing this, a valuable lesson is prevented. In such a case a father may properly explain that pen-knives cost money, and that to get money requires labour; that he cannot afford to purchase new pen-knives for one who loses or breaks them; and that, until he sees evidence of greater carefulness, he must decline to make good the loss. A parallel discipline will serve to check extravagances. (p. 121.)

The advantages of letting every misdemeanour be followed by its natural inconvenience or penalty are three in number:—(1.) Right conceptions of cause and effect are created in the mind. The child gains by degrees a knowledge of causation, and is prepared thereby for proper conduct in life; whereas in the case of a child whose punishments have merely consisted in the artificial ones of parental or tutorial displeasure, it is found that when the restraints of parents and tutors are removed, the youth plunges into every description of extravagance, and has to learn by experience the true restraints or natural reactions which found no place in his early training. (2.) This mode of discipline is one of pure justice, and will be recognised as such by every child. Suppose a boy is habitually reckless of his clothes, scrambles through hedges without caution, or is quite regardless of mud. If he is beaten or sent to bed, he is apt to consider himself ill-used, and is more likely to brood over his injuries than to repent of his transgressions. But suppose he is made to rectify the evil he has done—mend the tear in his garment, or clean off the mud adhering to it, will he not feel that the evil is one of his own producing? Will he not be quite conscious of the connexion between the penalty and the cause, and, recognizing the justice of the arrangement, will he not make a mental note to be more careful in future? If the boy shews obtuseness, if several suits of clothes are spoiled, the father, pursuing the same discipline of cause and effect, will decline to purchase new clothes till the ordinary time has elapsed, and meanwhile the boy is debarred from many pleasant excursions and from social gatherings, and in time can scarcely fail to perceive that his own carelessness has been at the root of his misfortunes. (3.) This system of discipline keeps the relationship between parents and children sweeter than it otherwise would be. There is no mutual anger, no ruffling of temper as in the ordinary artificial method of government, when parents make or unmake family laws at pleasure, and identify their own supremacy and dignity with the maintenance of these laws, every transgression being regarded as an offence against themselves, and a cause of anger on their part. There are no vexations arising from the parents taking upon themselves, in the shape of extra labour or cost, the evil consequences which should have been allowed to follow the wrong-doers. A father, who beats his boy for carelessly or wilfully breaking a sister's toy, and then himself pays for a new toy, inflicts an artificial penalty on the transgressor, and takes the natural penalty on himself, his own feelings and those of the transgressor being alike needlessly irritated. If he told the boy that a new toy must be bought from his pocket-money, this would be far less heart-burning, and the boy would at the same time experience the equitable and salutary consequence of his misdeed. Mutual exasperations being thus prevented, a much happier and a more influential relation springs up between parent and child.

These simple cases shew sufficiently the beauty of what Spencer calls the 'divinely-ordained method' of moral education. But he does not rest here, but goes on to discuss the higher and more subtle applications of the system. What is to be done in cases of more serious misconduct? How is this plan to be carried out when a petty theft has been committed, or when a lie has been told? Before replying to these questions, Spencer illustrates the beneficial effects resulting from kindly relations between parents and children, and remarks that if these relations were what they should be, serious offences would be reduced to a minimum. At present this is far from being the case, the general treatment of children oscillating between petting and scolding, between gentleness and castigation. A mother commonly thinks it sufficient to tell her little boy that she is his best friend, and, assuming that he ought to believe her, concludes that he will do so. 'It is all for your good.' 'I know what is proper for you better than you do yourself.' 'You are not old enough to understand it now, but when you grow up you will thank me for doing what I do.' These, and like assertions, are daily reiterated. Meanwhile the boy is daily suffering positive penalties, and is hourly forbidden to do this, that, and the other thing, which he wishes to do. By words he hears that his happiness is the end in view; but by deeds he finds that pain is his portion in the meantime. Naturally he becomes sceptical as to his mother's professions of friendship, and one can hardly blame him, for would not the mother reason in the same way if placed in similar circumstances? If among her acquaintances she found some one who was constantly thwarting her wishes, uttering sharp reprimands, and occasionally inflicting actual penalties on her, she would pay small attention to any professions of anxiety for her welfare which accompanied these acts. (p. 129.) How different the result would be, 'if the 'divinely-ordained method' were pursued; in which the mother not only avoids becoming the instrument of punishment, but plays the part of a friend by warning her child of the punishment which nature will inflict. Suppose the child with inquisitive promptings is burning pieces of paper in the candle and watching the effect. A mother of the unreflective type will, on the plea of keeping him from mischief, or from fear that he will burn himself, order him to desist; and, if he refuses, snatch the paper from him. But a mother with brains will reason thus: 'If I put a stop to this, I shall prevent the acquirement of a certain amount of knowledge. It is true that I may save the child from a burn, but what then? He is sure to burn himself sometime, and it is absolutely necessary that he should learn sooner or later the properties of flame, and he will probably come to learn them at greater risk and with greater pain than he may do now, when I am present. To save him now from a hurt which he cannot conceive, and which has therefore no existence for him, I hurt him in a way which he feels keenly enough, and so become from his point of view, a minister of evil. My best course, then, is simply to warn him of the danger, and to be ready to prevent any serious damage.' She contents herself, therefore, with saying, 'I fear you will hurt yourself if you do that.' The boy perseveres and ends by burning his hand—with what results? He has gained experience which he must have gained sooner or later; and he has found that his mother's warning was meant for his good; he has therefore a further proof of her benevolence, and of her judgment, a further reason for loving her. (p. 130.)

The only exception I should take to Spencer's recommendation in this case or any other attended with danger to a child is this: the mother, in the case supposed, is near the child, and no serious hurt can befall him; but suppose that at this time he does not hurt himself, and the next time he plays with fire his mother should be absent, what serious accident might not happen? Spencer, of course, recommends that when there is danger to life and limb, forcible prevention must be adopted. A three-year-old urchin playing with an open razor cannot be allowed to learn by this discipline of consequences, for the consequences may be too serious. But, leaving out extreme cases, we should pursue the system, not of guarding a child from the small risks which it daily runs, but that of advising and warning it against them. Instead of being told in words, which deeds seem to contradict, that their parents are their best friends, children will learn this truth by a consistent daily experience, and so learning it will acquire a degree of trust and attachment which nothing else can give.

The bearing which all this has on the disposal of graver offences is a most important one, for graver offences are reduced to a minimum under this *régime*. When such offences do occur, however, as they will occasionally occur, even under the best system, the discipline of natural consequences should still be resorted to. In the case of a theft we must consider what its natural consequences are. They are of two kinds—direct and indirect; restitution of the thing stolen, or the giving of an equivalent, and the grave displeasure of parents, which will be potent for good in proportion to the warmth of attachment existing between parent and child; and few will question the fact that the pain of the second may be more intense than that of the first, for who has not regarded as a serious misfortune long and keenly regretted by him, the displeasure of an admired and cherished friend? Spencer, who is more suggestive than exhaustive, does not take any further case, but leaves the disposal of other offences, such as cruelty, lying, and swearing, to the student's ingenuity.

Spencer concludes his essay on moral education by a few practical maxims and rules: First, do not expect from a child any great amount of moral goodness, for our higher moral faculties are comparatively late in their evolution, and an early activity, produced by stimulation, will be at the expense of the future character. Children who were models of juvenile goodness often end by being below par in riper years; and on the other hand exemplary men are often the issue of a childhood by no means promising. Be content, therefore, with moderate measures and moderate results. Have patience with your child's imperfections, and you will be less prone to that constant scolding and threatening and forbidding, by which many parents induce a chronic domestic irritation, in the foolish hope that they will thus make their children what they should be. Second, satisfy yourself with seeing that your child always suffers the natural consequences of his actions; leave him, whenever you can, to the discipline of experience, and pause in each case of transgression to consider what is the natural consequence, and how it may best be brought home to the transgressor. You must be careful at the same time to shew your approbation or disapprobation in a marked way, for while parental displeasure and its artificial penalties should never be *substituted* for natural penalties, it should invariably *accompany* them. Such amount of sorrow or indignation as you feel should be expressed in words or manner, subject of course to the approval of your judgment. Third, be sparing of commands. Command only when other means are inapplicable or have failed. 'In frequent orders the parent's advantage is more considered than the child's,' says Richter. Fourth, but whenever you *do* command, command with decision and consistency. If the case is one which really cannot be otherwise dealt with, then issue your fiat, and having issued it, never afterwards swerve from it. Let your penalties be like the penalties inflicted by inanimate nature —inevitable. The hot cinder burns a child the first time he seizes it; it burns him the second time; it burns him the third time; it burns him every time; and he very soon learns not to touch the hot cinder. If you are equally consistent; if the consequences which you tell your child will follow specified acts, follow with like uniformity, he will soon come to respect your laws as he does those of nature. (p. 139.) Fifth, remember that the aim of your discipline should be to produce a *self-governing* being; not to produce a being to be *governed by others*. Your children are meant to be freemen not slaves, and it is your duty to accustom them to self-control, while they are still under your eye. The history of domestic rule should typify the history of our political rule; at the outset, autocratic control, where control is really needful; by and bye an incipient constitutionalism, in which the liberty of the subject gains some express recognition; successive extensions of this liberty of the subject gradually ending in parental abdication (p. 140), an advice which is in other words identical with Locke's. Lastly, always recollect that to educate rightly is not a simple and easy thing, but a complex and extremely difficult thing. If you would carry out with success a rational and civilized system, you must be prepared for considerable mental exertion, for some study, some ingenuity, some patience, some self-control. You will have habitually to consider what are the results which in adult life follow certain kinds of acts; and you must then devise methods by which parallel results shall be entailed on the parallel acts of your children. Especially if you are dealing with children who have been wrongly treated, you must be prepared for a lengthened trial of patience, before succeeding with better methods, since that which is not easy, where a right state of feeling has been established from the beginning, becomes doubly difficult when a wrong state of feeling has to be set right. (p. 142.) This advice is well suited to teachers. In brief, you will have to carry on your own higher education at the same time that you are educating your children. Intellectually, you must cultivate to good purpose that most complex of subjects—human nature, and its laws, as exhibited in your children, in yourself, and in the world. Morally, you must keep in constant exercise your higher feelings and restrain your lower. It is a truth yet remaining to be recognized that the last stage in the mental development of each man and woman is only to be reached through a proper discharge of the parental duties. The method of education thus proposed, though it calls for much labour and self-sacrifice, yet promises an abundant return of happiness immediate and remote; for, as Spencer observes, a good system is twice blessed; it blesses him that trains, and him that's trained.

Thus closes, 'not only one of the most readable, but also one of the most important books on education in the English language.'

INDEX.

Activities of human life, . 244
Æsop's Fables, ... 34
Agricultural Schools, . . 212
Arithmetic (Locke), . . . 40
,, (Pestalozzi), . . 94
,, (Lancaster), . . 157
,, (Stow), . . . 213
Arnold, Dr., on Public Schools, ... 12
Art of Teaching (Locke), . 31
,, (Pestalozzi), . . 118
,, (Wilderspin), 170, 180
,, (Spencer), . . 265

Ball-frame, ... 182
Bell, Dr. Andrew, see Table of Contents.
Biber on Mutual Instruction, 79
Bible (Locke), ... 47
,, (Lancaster), . . . 160
,, (Wilderspin), . . . 182
,, (Stow), . . . 202, 208
,, Picturing out, . . . 220
,, Reading, ... 202
,, Teaching, ... 202
,, Training, . . 202, 206
,, Training Lesson, . . 208
Book-keeping (Locke), . . 40
,, (Stow), . . 214
British and Foreign School Society, ... 146
Buchanan, Mr., the First Infant Master, ... 167

Chairs of Education, . . 148
Children, Behaviour of, . . 21
,, Curiosity of, . . 30
,, Locke's love for, 6
Classification, ... 227
,, of human activities, 244
Committing to Memory, . 36
Composition (Locke), . . 41
Corporal Punishment—
 (Locke), 22, 23
 ,, (Bell), . . 137
Cowper on Public Schools, 11
Criticism lessons, . . . 193

De Fellenberg, ... 100
Discipline (Locke), . . . 19
,, (Dr. Bell), . . 133
,, (Lancaster), . . 159
,, (Wilderspin), . 179
,, (Spencer), . . 283
,, of Natural Consequences, . . 285
Donaldson, Dr., on the Monitorial System, ... 139
Drawing (Locke), . . . 39
,, (Pestalozzi), . . 93
,, (Spencer), . . . 279
Dunn, Mr., on Monitorial System, ... 141

Edgeworth, Miss, 125, 284, note.
Education, Infant (Pestalozzi), 73
,, (Wilderspin), 179

INDEX.

Education, Infant (Spencer), 276
Education, Intellectual—
         (Stow), . . 201
,,   (Spencer), . 265
,,   Mixed (Stow), . 228
,,   Moral (Locke), 19, 25
,,   ,, (Pestalozzi), 80
,,   ,, (Spencer), 283, 295
,,   Physical (Locke), . 17
,,   ,, (Bell), . 135
,,   ,, (Stow), . 236
,,   ,, (Spencer), 248
"Evening Hour of a Hermit," 65
"Experiment on Education,"
    (Dr. Bell), ... 127

Fichte, ... 104
Fitch, Mr., on Monitorial
    System, ... 140
Flattery (Locke), . . . 27
French (Locke), ... 43

Gallery Lessons, ... 209
,,   Moral Training in, . 232
Geography, ... 281
,,   (Pestalozzi), . 99
Geometry, ... 272
Glasgow Education Society, 190
Grammar (Locke), . . . 41
,,   (Stow), . . 223
,,   (Spencer), . . 266

Health, Locke's Rules on, . 18
History for Children, . . 257
Home and Colonial Society, 184
"How Gertrude teaches her
    Children," . . 78, 86, 97

Industrial School (Pestalozzi), 61
Infant Education ,, 73
,,   (Wilderspin), 179
,,   (Spencer), . 276
Infant Schools, origin of, . 166
,,   organization of, 171
Infant School Society—
,, (Home and Colonial), 184
,, (London), . . . 171

Infant Teachers, qualifications of, ... 179
Intellectual Education—
    (Spencer), 265
,,   (Stow), . 201

Johnson, Dr. Samuel, . . 199

Kindergarten System, . . 181
Knowledges, relative value of, 259

Lancaster, Joseph, see Table
    of Contents.
Lancaster's School, . . . 153
Language, Exercises in, . 91
Languages versus Science, . 259
Latin (Locke), ... 45
Learning should be interesting (Locke), . . 32
,,   (Wilderspin), 183
,,   (Spencer), . 280
Learning by rote, . 241, 266
Leibnitz on Locke's
    "Thoughts," 4
Locke, John, see Table of
    Contents.
"Leonard and Gertrude,". 68
Letterwriting (Locke), . . 42

Madras System, ... 127
Marcel, M., quoted, . 266, 267
"Measure of Value" in
    Knowledge, ... 242
Mental Evolution, . . . 267
Mixed System, . . 177, 228
Monitor, the First, . . . 123
Monitorial System—
    (Pestalozzi), ... 78
,, (Biber), ... 79
,, (Dr. Bell), ... 127
,, (Lancaster), ... 156
,, (Stow), ... 237
,, (Dr. Donaldson), . . 139
,, (Mr. Fitch), ... 140
,, (Professor Pillans), . . 141
,, (Mr. Dunn), ... 141
,, Applied to Agriculture, 163

INDEX. 301

Montaigne on "Learning by rote,". 266
Moral Discipline (Locke), 19, 25
,, (Dr. Bell), . . 133
,, (Lancaster), . . 159
,, (Spencer), . . 283
,, Rules for, . . . 295
Moral Training (Pestalozzi), 80
,, (Wilderspin), 177
,, (Stow), . . 232
,, in gallery, . 232
Morf's Pestalozzi, . 120, *note*.
Museums for Schools, . . 213

National Society, ... 145
Nature to be followed in Education (Pestalozzi), . 66
,, (Wilderspin), . 180
,, (Spencer), . . 267
Nature, teachings of, 245, 274, 284
Normal School, the first, . 191
,, Glasgow Free Church, 197
Nursery Legislation, . . . 253

Oberlin, ... 166
Oberlin College, ... 230
Object Lessons (Pestalozzi), 82
,, (Professor Moseley), 83
,, (Raumer), . . . 113
,, (Spencer), . . 277
Observing powers, culture of, 182, 196, 274
Organization (Dr. Bell), . 127
,, (Wilderspin), . 171

Paidometer, ... 138
Perspective, ... 271
Pestalozzi, Henry, *see* Table of Contents.
Physical Education (Locke), 17
,, (Bell), . 135
,, (Stow), . 236
,, (Spencer), 248
Physiology, ... 247
Pictures, ... 183
Picturing-out, ... 215

Pillans, Professor, on Monitorial System, ... 141
Pitt, Education of, . . . 13
Play-ground, moral training in, ... 177, 232
,, Superintendence in, 235
Poetry, Learning of, . . . 37
Praise (Locke), ... 29
Principles of Teaching, . . 268
Private Education, . . . 8
Public Schools, evils of, . 10
,, Cowper on, . . . 11
,, Dr. Arnold on, . 12
,, Suggestions on, 14, 231
Punishments (Locke), . . 28
,, (Bell), . . . 133
,, (Lancaster), . 159
,, (Spencer), . 288

Quick, Mr., quoted, 68, 252, 282

Raikes, Robert, ... 187
Ramsauer on Pestalozzi, 89, 95, 109
Raumer, Carl Von, . . . 105
,, on Pestalozzi, . 112
Reading (Locke), . . . 33
,, (Bell), ... 138
,, (Lancaster), . . 157
,, Bible, ... 202
,, without intelligence, 204
Religious Teaching (Locke), 47
,, (Lancaster), . 160
,, (Wilderspin), 182
,, (Stow), 202, 208
Rewards (Locke), . . . 27
,, (Lancaster), . . 159

Sabbath Schools, ... 187
School Museums, ... 213
Science Lessons, ... 209
,, Teaching, . . . 250
,, Benefits of, . . . 250
,, of Education, . . 268
Science *versus* Classics, . 259
Seeley, Professor, quoted, . 282
Shaftesbury, Earls of, . . 3

INDEX.

Simpson, Mr., on Wilderspin, ... 185
Simultaneous Teaching—
    (Pestalozzi), 78
  ,, (Stow), . . 227
Sociology, ... 255
Spencer, Herbert, *see* Table of Contents.
Stewart, Dugald, on Locke's "Thoughts," 49
Stow, David, *see* Table of Contents.
Syllabification (Dr. Bell), . 138
  ,, (Lancaster), . 157
Sympathy of Numbers, . . 225

Teacher, estimate of a—
    (Pestalozzi's), . 118
  ,, (Bell's), . . 129
  ,, (Wilderspin's), 179
  ,, (Spencer's), . 265

Teaching, Golden Rule in, . 137
Training System—
    (Wilderspin), 176
  ,, (Stow), . . 198
Training Lessons, 208, 209, 220
Translation, ... 46, 47
Trial by Jury, . . . 134, 233
Trimmer, Mrs., ... 143
Tutor, Locke's estimate of a, 14

Verses, Latin, ... 46

Weights and Measures, 183, 269
Wilderspin, Samuel, *see* Table of Contents.
Words and Things—
    (Pestalozzi), . 84
  ,, (Wilderspin), 180
Writing (Locke), ... 37
  ,, on sand, 123, 137, 156
Wyse, Mr., quoted, . 266, 268

GLASGOW:
PRINTED AT THE UNIVERSITY PRESS.

RECENTLY PUBLISHED BY

JAMES MACLEHOSE, GLASGOW.

Second Edition, extra fcap. 8vo, price 7s., cloth.

BORLAND HALL: a Poem in Six Books. By the Author of "Olrig Grange."

"Lyell's mother, stern and unrepentant, even in death, is a terrible portrait. .... We recognize the genius of the author of 'Olrig Grange' in the stinging sarcasm with which she combats his hesitation, and the hard straightforwardness with which she rejects his caresses, and speaks of her own crime. .... The author portrays with wonderful insight and refinement the tempest of doubt, the angry turbulence of feeling, and the bitter, aching, desperate misery of this poor soul, driven into darkness by another's sin, having lost its hold on faith and truth. . . . . Such a poem as this will surely have a distinct influence over social thought and custom, for the lessons inculcated have the added weight and enforcement of a style singularly brilliant and passionately fervent, a verse melodious and various in measure, a command of language unusually extensive and apt, and an exquisite sensibility to all natural loveliness."—*English Independent.*

Second Edition, extra fcap. 8vo, price 6s., cloth.

SONGS AND FABLES. By WILLIAM J. MACQUORN RANKINE, late Professor of Civil Engineering in the University of Glasgow. With Portrait, and with 10 Illustrations by J. B. (MRS. HUGH BLACKBURN).

"His happiest vein is one of mingled sentiment and irony; but his ballads have the force, the roughness, the directness without which it is impossible for a ballad to be genuinely popular. The subject of 'They never shall have Gibraltar' is antiquated; but even a reader who has never heard of Goldwin Smith's advice to us to drop Gibraltar to Spain, as we dropped the Ionian Islands to Greece, to satisfy an even emptier historico-national sentiment, can appreciate the patriotic fire of the ballad. We do not indulge ourselves so far as to quote it, or 'The Engine-driver to his Engine,' which has equally the stamp of genius, or the famous 'Three-foot Rule' which was published in our own columns by a correspondent immediately after his death. The 'Infant Metaphysician' is a capital specimen of his irony, and the 'Ode in praise of the City of Mullingar' might have claimed quotation if it had not happened too vividly to recall similar triumphs of the genius of Thackeray and Father Prout. It may be from professional sympathies, but we find few things in the volume better than 'Loyal Peter,' which brings back the memory of old Peter Mackenzie, of the *Glasgow Reformers' Gazette.*"—*Glasgow Herald.*

Second Edition, extra fcap. 8vo, price 6s. 6d., cloth.

OLRIG GRANGE: a Poem in Six Books. Edited by HERMANN KUNST, Philol. Professor.

"The story itself is very simple, but it is told in powerful and suggestive verse. The composition is instinct with quick and passionate feeling to a degree that attests the truly poetic nature of the man who produced it. It exhibits much more of genuine thought, of various knowledge, of regulated and exquisite sensibility. The author exhibits a fine and firm discrimination of character, a glowing and abundant fancy, a subtile eye to read the symbolism of nature, and great wealth and mastery of language, and he has employed it for worthy purposes."—*Spectator.*

New and Enlarged Edition, extra fcap. 8vo, price 6s., cloth.

THE POETICAL WORKS OF DAVID GRAY.

Edited by HENRY GLASSFORD BELL, late Sheriff of Lanarkshire.

"This volume possesses a peculiarity, independent of the gems which it embodies, in that the editing of it was the last literary labour of the late lamented Sheriff of Lanarkshire. The reverential vigour which pervades the equable verses of David Gray is, however, unique; there is a more forcible beauty in his pieces than in those of the Westmoreland poet, and the awe he manifested 'for things unseen and eternal' is quite as conspicuous as the deep and steady devotion of the poet of the 'Seasons.' The volume is got up with sufficient taste not to befool the precious things within."—*Edinburgh Courant.*

In 1 vol., small 8vo, price 6s. 6d., cloth.

THE TWEED AND OTHER POEMS.

By JOHN VEITCH, LL.D., Professor of Logic and Rhetoric in the University of Glasgow.

"Evidently the poem is the genuine outcome of a life—the embodiment of the sight and sounds he has longest known and most loved—of the thoughts most habitual to him, of the feelings that lie deepest within him. . . . The poet knows and loves Tweedside so well that no feature of the landscape, however minute, not a mist or wind that wanders over it, but is precious to his eye, invested with an importance which he can hardly expect a stranger fully to appreciate. In this entire devotion to his subject lies the poet's strength. . . Every hillside, and 'scaur,' and 'hope,' is described with the utmost reverential fidelity to the exact truth of things."—*Scotsman.*

"We have here a poem finely conceived, wrought out with a force and grace that, if not of the highest order, are certainly both admirable and uncommon. . . . Rich in picturesque descriptions, and instinct with a sentiment that appeals to the universal heart of humanity. . . . Several of the Ballads seem to us to be in their different veins as exquisite a reproduction of the genuine romantic ballads, native to the region from early times, as we have ever met."—*Daily Review.*

In extra fcap. 8vo, price 5s., cloth.

HILLSIDE RHYMES. By PROFESSOR VEITCH.

"Let any one who cares for fine reflective poetry read for himself and judge. Besides the solid substance of thought which pervades it, he will find here and there those quick insights, those spontaneous felicities of language which distinguish the man of natural power from the man of mere cultivation. . . . Next to an autumn day among the hills themselves, commend us to poems like these, in which so much of the finer breath and spirit of those pathetic hills is distilled into melody."—*Scotsman.*

1 vol., crown 8vo, price 7s. 6d., cloth.

SERMONS PREACHED IN TRINITY

CHURCH, GLASGOW. By WILLIAM PULSFORD, D.D.

"The Sermons have much of the brilliancy of thought and style by which Robertson fascinated his Brighton hearers."—*Daily Review.*

"The preacher, we are made to feel, speaks to us out of the fulness of his own spiritual and intellectual life. He has been under no temptation to borrow, just because he had a message of his own to deliver. . . . He is a preacher because he has been first a thinker."—*Spectator.*

JAMES MACLEHOSE, GLASGOW.

www.ingramcontent.com/pod-product-compliance
Lightning Source LLC
Chambersburg PA
CBHW030754230426
43667CB00007B/964